A PHOTOGRAPHIC HI

Eton Wick & Eton

Eton Wick History Group

Published by
Robert Boyd Publications
260 Colwell Drive
Witney, Oxfordshire OX8 7LW

First published 2000

ISBN: 1 899536 50 7

Printed and bound by The Alden Group, Oxford and Northampton

Contents

Dear Reader,

Apart from Dr. Judith Hunter's book *The Story of a Village. Eton Wick 1217–1977*, there has been no other general work on the community until this, the year of the Millennium. Every effort has been taken to ensure that the facts, dates and identifications in this book are as accurate as possible. Nevertheless, we acknowledge that the discerning reader may be able to offer corrections or additional information. We would welcome your help in updating our records.

We hope you enjoy this book, and that its contents will provide an interesting insight into our community.

The Authors

Windsor Castle from Victoria Road, Eton Wick.

This photograph was taken in 1947. It looks eastwards to the Castle over Meux's Field (then the Shepherds Hut public house paddock), allotments at the rear of the Village Hall, the recreation ground, and then South Field to the Great Western Railway viaduct. The houses of Princes Close now cover most of Meux's Field and the Windsor and Eton Relief Road obscures the railway viaduct.

Acknowledgements

The Eton Wick History Group would like to express its appreciation to the following:

The Royal Albert Institute Trust and the Millennium Festival 'Awards for All' Fund for their financial help.

The Leicestershire Records Office for permission to reproduce the photographs taken by George Henton.

Mr A B Demaus for permission to reproduce the photographs taken by his father, the Rev. Demaus.

The many other people who have generously supplied photographs: Mr John Austin, Mrs Joan Ballhatchet, Mr George Birch, Mrs and Miss Campion, Mr William Cooley, Mr Tony Cullum, Mr John Denham, Mrs Margaret Everitt, Mr David Gibson, Mrs Mary Gyngell, Mrs Pat Hodge, Dr Judith Hunter, Mrs Brenda Irvin, Mrs Joan Neighbour, Mrs Rita Pidgeon, Mrs Margaret Springford, Mr Cyril Tarrant, Mr Jamie Tarrant, Mrs Olive Tarrant, Mrs Rene Thompson and Mrs Jean Tyler.

To Mrs Joan Ballhatchet, Mrs Mary Gyngell and Mrs Teresa Stanton our thanks for proof reading the text throughout.

The many other people and organisations who have helped with local knowledge and assistance with this book including:

The Over 60s Club, The Women's Institute, The Village Hall Committee, and the local Libraries and Press.

The Group would also like to record their thanks to their colleagues Mr Peter Tarrant for compiling the publication, Mr Jonathan Palmer for his assistance and guidance in its printing and distribution, and to Mr Frank Bond, who collated the great majority of the photographs and without whose enthusiasm the project would probably not have been executed.

We have made every effort to establish copyright where appropriate and to obtain permission to reproduce, but if we have inadvertently omitted to do so in any particular instance we offer our sincere apologies.

Foreword

Eton Wick and Eton have Anglo-Saxon names, so it is reasonable to think of their origins as being about one thousand years ago. However, it has been only for some hundred years, since the invention of the photographic image, that we have had the benefit of a completely accurate pictorial record of the community and local events. The History Group is fortunate in having a considerable number of old photographs amongst its records. The oldest photograph at the time of preparing this book was taken in 1885 and is of Boveney Lock; there are several pictures of the floods of 1894, and of local rural scenes taken by artist George Henton in 1894/95 (courtesy of Leicestershire Records Office) and some by the Rev. Demaus (Eton Wick curate 1898–1900), plus a large number donated from local family albums. Many of these old photographs appear in this book. There is a greater proportion of pictures relating to the village than of Eton town because the book has been produced by the Eton Wick History Group, largely financed by a Millennium Fund grant which was awarded for this express purpose; also much has already been written about 'town and gown'.

For hundreds of years the village depended largely on the town and college for employment and trade. Fuel and produce was supplied to the town before the coming of Eton College in the mid-15th century, and to both town and college later. School boys were educated at Eton Porny School until 1939 when Slough and Eton (C of E) Secondary School in Ragstone Road, Chalvey, was built. By the end of the 20th century, the development of Slough Trading Estate and other industries and services, and the vast improvements in transport had virtually severed this historic link.

Little more than one century ago, when those first local photographs were being taken of the village, Eton Wick was being spoken and written of as a hamlet. Perhaps a fair description, as in 1841 there were only 62 houses in the village, and as recorded in Dr Judith Hunter's excellent book *The Story of a Village. Eton Wick 1217–1977*, this was three times the number existing 40 years earlier. These early dwellings were built on the marginally higher ground to the north of today's village; perhaps not noticeably much higher, but occupiers of those houses would testify to the importance of the extra inches during years of flood. Some villagers can still remember March 1947, when many homes were flooded, and yet the farm houses to the north, although surrounded by the flood waters, remained high and dry.

The growth of Eton Wick came about in spasmodic bursts and was always influenced and restricted by Lammas regulations and the parish boundary. The areas south and east of the village were Lammas and Common lands, just as they are today. Land to the west of Bell Lane was in the parish of Burnham and much of it belonged to the Palmer family of Dorney, or was part of Bell Farm. Bell Farm House itself lies just east of the boundary. The cottages built mainly for the farm workers, Bell Cottages and Bell Farm Cottages, were across the boundary in Burnham parish (it is said that the latter Cottages straddled the boundary line). It is likely at this time, in the mid-19th century, that the only other dwelling west of Bell Lane was the Shepherds Hut public house.

In the 18th and 19th centuries, most of the village development was along Common Road between Wheatbutts Field and Sheepcote Road, which was then only a gated muddy farm track. These early cottages had very long gardens or smallholdings, stretching in most cases from the building itself to today's main Eton Wick Road. The buildings backed onto Common Road, giving ready access to the stream and ponds, and the common, on which many inhabitants and their livestock depended. A few exceptions, built on the main road, included the Three Horseshoes public house and a terrace of ten small dwellings called Prospect Place (built 1833), with their gardens running down to the common. By the mid-19th century, the village population had risen from 100 to 300. Numbers were to increase in the 1860s when the long gardens and other available infill sites were built on. Many of these houses can be seen along the main road today, with construction date plaques on them such as Palmer Place, St Leonard's Place, etc.

By 1880 the population of Eton Wick was approximately 500, but there was now very little land available within the old village for further growth. The next big surge of building came in the 1880s to 1890s, west of the Parish of Eton Wick, when land formerly part of Bell Farm was made available for housing development. The residential area was known as Boveney New Town, and comprised of Alma, Inkerman and North Field Roads. It had its own parish council, and soon housed a population of 500, equalling that of Eton Wick parish. Both Parish Councils were then independent of Eton, and the two communities were conscious of their own identities, although very much inter-dependent. Later, new organisations and infrastructures adopted the combined two-parish title; for example Eton Wick and Boveney Scouts, Eton Wick and Boveney War Memorial and Eton Wick and Boveney Institute (later renamed the Village Hall). In addition to this new development north of the main Eton Wick Road, a few houses were built along the main road in the 1890s, and to the south, Sir Charles Palmer of Dorney developed a long row of terraced houses in Victoria Road.

Possibly the biggest incremental step in population came between World War II and the late 1960s, by which time the population was approaching 3000. Much of the post-war building development was carried out by the Eton Urban District Council (Eton Wick, which by now included Boveney New Town, lost its independent council in 1934). The new building covered Tilstone Field, the allotments which laid between Moore's Lane and the cattle gate to Dorney Common. Privately owned dwellings were built on orchards and pigsties south of Victoria Road and Tilstone; older dwellings along Common and Sheepcote Roads were demolished to make way for houses and flats, bringing the population to much the same size as it is today.

An important feature of Eton Wick has always been its surrounding Common and Lammas lands, the Rights of which have been jealously guarded over the years. In 1965 these lands were registered under the Commons Registration Act and it is only with the consent of the Secretary of State for the Environment that such lands can be released for development.

Frank Bond
Chairman, Eton Wick History Group

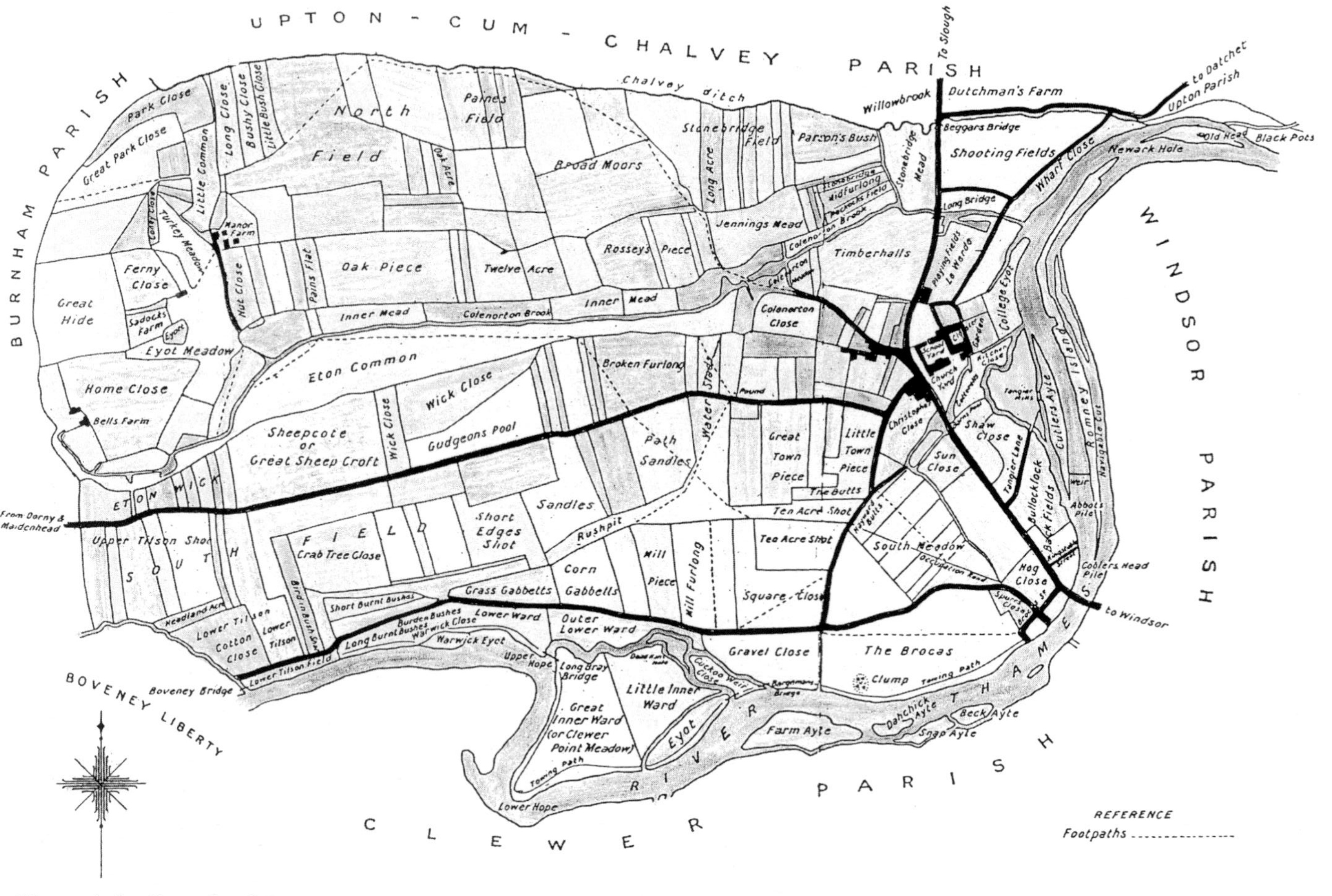

Plan of the Parish of Eton-cum-Stockdale and Colenorton in the County of Buckingham, late 19th century.

Agriculture and Farm Houses

Bell Farm House

This photograph of Bell Farm House, taken at the turn of the 19th century, shows farm manager Charles Tough with a shot gun on his lap and a black gun dog sitting at his feet. Presumably the shot gun is pointing somewhere between his wife Annie seated opposite, and the unidentified man seated in the doorway. Charles and Annie came to Eton Wick from Kent. Charles had been appointed by the Council to manage their recently acquired farm, the fields of which were primarily to be used as the Eton Sewage Farm. Annie was the major driving force behind the building of the Methodist Chapel in nearby Alma Road in 1886.

Bell Farm House was the home of several generations of the Bell family, who were major property owners and farmers in and around the district during the 16th and 17th centuries. The house is circa 1360 in origin and is timber framed with brick infilling. There have been many alterations over the centuries. In the mid-1850s, the south elevation was tile hung and a Victorian porch replaced the gabled mediaeval bell tower. It is a Grade II* Listed Building.

The 14th century Granary belonging to Bell Farm House was converted to living accommodation in 1963. As part of the conversion the pigsties beneath the granary (see top photograph) were made into garages. Bricks were turned weather face inside, and the whole timber frame raised to comply with Building Regulations.

ETON WICK, NEAR WINDSOR, BERKS.

EXCELLENT FREEHOLD FARM,

AND

TWENTY COTTAGES WITH LARGE GARDEN TO EACH,

And valuable Common Rights,

IN THE PARISHES OF ETON AND BOVENEY, BUCKS.

TO BE SOLD BY AUCTION,

By Mr. TEBBOTT,

AT THE SWAN INN WINDSOR,

On Tuesday, the 25th of September, at One o'clock.

IN LOTS, WITH EARLY POSSESSION,

Under the direction of the Devisees in Trust and Executors of the late Mr. JOHN ATKINS, of Chalvey, Bucks, deceased,

A CAPITAL FREEHOLD ESTATE, called "BELL'S FARM," in the occupation of Mrs. Atkins, situate at Eton Wick, a short distance from, and on the right-hand side of the road leading from Eton to Dorney; comprising about 70 acres of remarkably Rich Meadow and Arable Land, (part old enclosed and part Lammas) in the highest state of cultivation, possessing valuable common rights, and bounded by Property of the Crown, Sir Charles Palmer, C. T. Depree, John Penn, and T. Williams, Esqrs., with a Farm House standing nearly in the centre of its grounds, and a capital Garden, about an acre and a half, abundantly stocked with choice fruit trees, bounded on one side by a stream of fine water; a very compact Farm Yard, with two large barns, stabling for four horses, nag stable, chaise house, spacious open shed, an excellent granary on brick piers, and various other buildings applicable for agricultural purposes. The situation is particularly dry and airy, and its contiguity to the towns of Windsor and Eton, the great Western Road, and three great Market Towns, will be found worthy of notice either for occupation or investment; Two Labourers' Cottages, with gardens, on the road side, leading to the farm, in the occupation of William Parker and — Newell, at 10*l.* 8*s.* per annum; TEN newly brick-built and slated COTTAGES, called "PROSPECT PLACE," fronting to the Dorney road, with two rooms and a large garden to each, at 6*l.* 10*s.* per annum, in the occupation of William Croxford and others; a very desirable piece of Land adjoining, with about 130 feet frontage, now in the occupation of Mrs. Atkins; and two cottages and Gardens, at the back of ditto, opening upon Eton Common, in the occupation of Thomas Davis and William Wansell, at 7*l.* 10*s.* each; a Piece of Garden Ground abutting on the farm house of John Penn, Esq., in the occupation of Mrs. Lillywhite, at 6*l.* 6*s.* per annum; a Brick and Thatched Cottage, with garden, near to Mrs. Lillywhite's farm house, in the occupation of Thomas King, at 7*l.* 16*s.*; a fine Close of Old Meadow Land, with a Cottage, small barn, shed, and nearly three quarters of an acre of garden ground, presenting a frontage to Little Eton Common of 320 feet, in the occupation of James Deverell, at 27*l.* per annum; three Cottages nearly opposite, with large gardens, in the occupations of George Sola, William Bunce, and Francis Barfoot, at 23*l* 10*s.*; a cottage, with yard, small barn, and large garden, in the occupation of William Hale, at the yearly rental of 12*l.*

May be viewed by applying to William Cox, on the premises; and printed particulars, with a plan of the property, to be had 14 days previous to the sale, of Mr. Mears, Solicitor, Bagshot; Mr. Cotterell, Warfield, Mr. Marlin, Solicitor, Peascod-street, Windsor; Rose Inn, Wokingham; Crown, Reading; Rose and Crown, Hounslow; Hatchett's Hotel, Piccadilly; and at Mr. Tebbott's Office, Windsor.

A clipping for the sale of Bell Farm estate. The description of the properties that were then part of the estate (including Prospect Place) and the names of the occupiers makes interesting reading. The reference to 'newly built' Prospect Place dates this to the 1830s.

Dairy Farm

The earliest known deed for Dairy Farm House is dated 1704, but refers to previous owners, so the house is likely to be older than this. At that time the farm is recorded as comprising forty acres, which included Wheatbutts Field and the land on which Hope Cottages were later built. There were also five closes of arable and pasture land, and sixteen strips dispersed in North Field, the Hyde and Waterslades. Within a few decades, Dairy Farm had been reduced to a mere seventeen acres, the greater part being lost to other farms.

In the early 1900s when this picture was taken, the farm was run by Charles Nottage. Charles died in 1913. His son Arthur, together with Arthur's brother-in-law Edwin Ashman farmed the land through World War I. Nottage and Ashman were followed in the 1920s by Harry Blakiston Morris and his family. The eldest son, Ted Morris, was co-founder of the well-known Slough Builders Merchants Miller, Morris and Brooker.

Bob Bond (son of Roland Bond, the founder of R Bond & Sons, Contractors) bought Dairy Farm in the late 1930s and worked it (in addition to his role in the Contracting Company) until his death in 1975. It is no longer a farm. Some of the land and buildings have been developed as livery stables, and two houses have been built on the land fronting the western end of the Common.

Little Common Farm

This old timber framed farm house dates back to the 17th century. It is situated across the end of Common Road overlooking Eton Wick Little Common (the large Common nearer the village is Great Common). Very little land went with the farm, and it depended very much in the early years on common and Lammas land grazing. Occupants during the 20th century include Alf Tarrant who bought it from his father James for £1000 in the 1930s. When Alf died, Bill Cooley (senior) took the farm on from Alf's widow Charlotte (née Bunce). It is still farmed by Bill's son. The photograph is believed to have been taken in the 1950s.

The pond was later infilled to allow large modern farm machinery to turn into Manor Farm, which is just across the road to the right. The meadow to the left is part of Saddocks Farm. All three farm houses were built in close proximity and within view of each other.

Long Close House

No photographs of this old farm house in its original timber clad state have come to hand. The house is located some half a mile beyond Little Common Farm House, at the north east end of the Common, and borders on Manor Farm and North Field. By the mid-20th century it was no longer a farm, and the house was modernised and brick clad. Before the 1914/18 war until some time after, the Quarterman family ran it as a pig farm. In the mid-1930s the Tutt family used it as a home and smallholding. After the 1939/45 war, it became the home of Bridget Rogers, who ran her Long Close Riding Stables from there. Bridget was also associated with Windsor's Theatre Royal as a stage director.

Long Close's connection with the stage/film industry has continued up to the present time as the home and vehicle museum of Tony and Paul Oliver. Vehicles are hired out to cinema and television film makers. Among many items that have apppeared on screen are Lt. Gruber's 'little tank' and Rene's ice cream van (TV series ''allo, 'allo'), Roger Rabbit's auto, and military vehicles in the film 'Evita'. The museum is occasionally open to the public and attracts visitors from far afield.

Saddocks Farm

This photograph dates to around the 1930s, when it was farmed by Arthur Tarrant and his family. Robert 'Sadocke' farmed here in the 1500s. The farm house and its extensive garden is on the left. The farm house is mainly 19th century, but closer inspection of the bricks and other features of the west (left-hand) side of the house show this part to be very much older. The farm buildings are, from the left, stables, the cow (milking) shed, and a dutch barn. The much older barn beyond that was constructed of reclaimed timbers, possibly ex-ships, pitched shiplap boards on a low brick wall, and clay roof tiles. Much of the barn, and the roof tiles of Saddocks Farm Cottages (opposite the barn beyond the photo) was lost in the great gale of 1987. Since Elizabethan times, ownership of the property has passed several times between the Crown and Eton College. When the farm cottages were built, the farm was Crown Estate as depicted on the date tablet on the west cottage – 1868 with 'VR' and a Crown above. There are a number of architecturally similar cottages scattered around the farm estates in Windsor Great Park. A circular thatched corn rick can be seen in the rick yard on the right. Up to the 1960s, Eton Wick Cricket Club played on the meadow beyond the farm house. For many visiting sides it was a novel and popular venue, despite the long grass of the outfield, interspersed with cow pats and rabbit holes. The farm was re-acquired by Eton College around 1940.

Saddocks Farm House and Garden c1906

At this time, James and Julia Tarrant lived here, followed by one of their sons, Arthur, and his family. This photograph is of the south elevation of the house. Arthur's surviving sons Cyril and Reg (J A) can still recall the rose covered trellis archway along the garden path and the immaculate flower beds on the lawn beyond the hedge. At the height of their farming days, James and his sons ran Saddocks, Manor, Crown and Little Common farms. At the end of the 20th century, Crown Farm is still in the hands of Jamie Tarrant, son of Reg (H).

Manor Farm

The photograph below shows the Farm House, the origins of which date to the 1700s. John Penn is on record as having bought the Manor in 1793. The photograph on the next page shows the entrance to the farm yard from Common Road. Both were taken around the 1960s. The area of the pond in the photograph is on Saddocks Farm land; it extended under the fence to the Manor Farm side from where there was a shallow ditch running from Little Common Farm. The pond was a popular skating venue for villagers before it was infilled in the 1960s. In the 20th century, the farm has been occupied by Urquarts, Tarrants and Kinrosses.

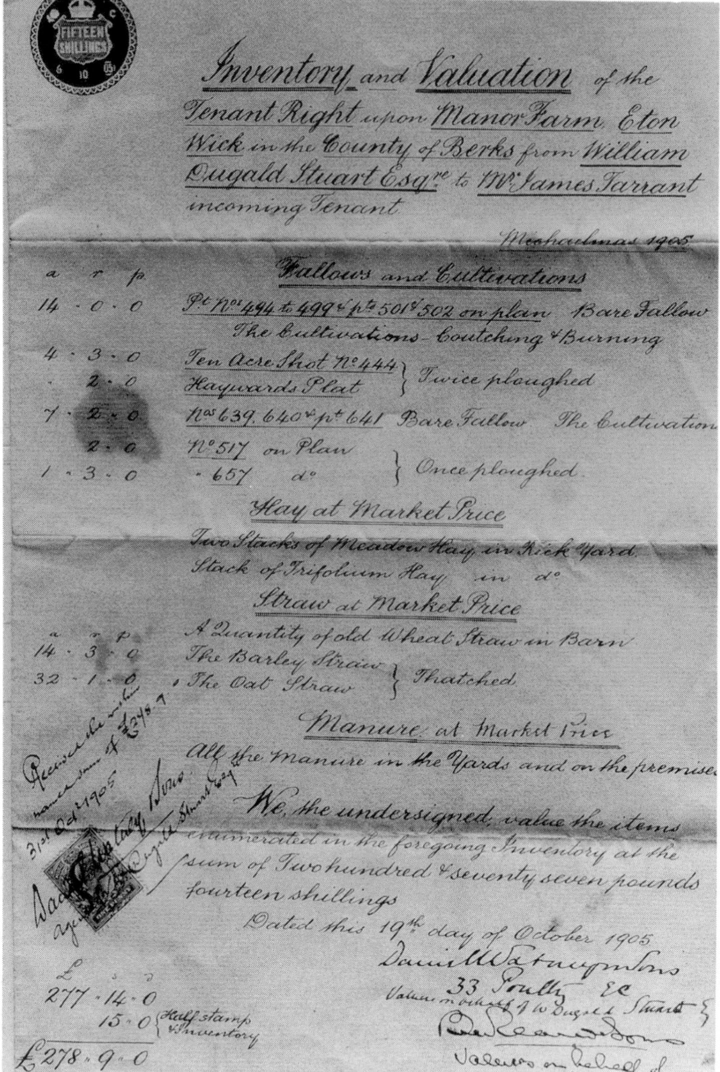

FIFTEEN SHILLINGS

Inventory and Valuation of the Tenant Right upon Manor Farm Eton Wick in the County of Berks from William Dugald Stuart Esqre to Mr James Tarrant incoming Tenant

Michaelmas 1905

Fallows and Cultivations

a r p	
14 . 0 . 0	Pt Nos 494 to 499 & pts 501 & 502 on plan Bare Fallow The Cultivations – Coutching & Burning
4 . 3 . 0	Ten Acre Shot No 444 } Twice ploughed
. 2 . 0	Haywards Plat }
7 . 2 . 0	Nos 639, 640 & pt 641 Bare Fallow The Cultivation
2 . 0	No 517 on Plan } Once ploughed
1 . 3 . 0	" 657 do }

Hay at Market Price

Two Stacks of Meadow Hay in Rick Yard

Stack of Trifolium Hay in do

Straw at Market Price

a r p	
	A Quantity of old Wheat Straw in Barn
14 . 3 . 0	The Barley Straw } Thatched
32 . 1 . 0	The Oat Straw }

Manure at Market Price

All the manure in the Yards and on the premises

We, the undersigned, value the items enumerated in the foregoing Inventory at the sum of Two hundred & seventy seven pounds fourteen shillings

Dated this 19th day of October 1905

David Watney & Sons
33 Poultry EC
Valuers on behalf of W Dugald Stuart Esq

[signature]
Valuers on behalf of

£	s	d	
277	14	0	
	15	0	Half stamp & Inventory
£278	9	0	

Received the within named sum of £278.9 ... 31st Oct 1905 ... agents for Dugald Stuart Esq

The Inventory of Manor Farm on change of tenancy from William Stuart (for the Crown) to James Tarrant, dated 19th December 1905.

Horse Sculpture 1997.

This life size sculpture by Fidel Garcia, was made at Manor Farm and erected in South Field between the Eton Wick Road and the river (along the tree line), where it stood for some weeks before succumbing to the weather, etc. It made an interesting relief to the otherwise featureless area of South Field.

Crown Farm

Crown Farm is situated some 400 m east of St John the Baptist Church, and lies between the Eton Wick Road and the Great Common, with access to both. The house is

believed to be early 17th century, with various alterations later in the same century. The west elevation is possibly timber framed and rough cast covered. The farm has been in the hands of several generations of the Tarrant family. It is still owned by Olive and Jamie (widow and son of Reginald H Tarrant). Surviving family members have seen Deeds for Crown Farm dated 1837 signed by a Robert Tarrant. A hand-written family record still exists in the hands of distant cousins in Utah, USA, referring to 'grandfather Philip Tarrant', born on the farm on Eton Wick Common in 1805' (although not necessarily Crown Farm). The upper photograph of the Farm House, from the family collection was professionally taken. The three young girls may well be Charlotte, Minnie and Rosie, daughters of James and Julia (great grandparents of the current Jamie) which would date the photo to the late 19th century. The lower photograph, taken about the 1960s, shows cows exiting the farm to the common.

To the east of Crown Farm there were originally other old farm dwellings. Among these were Common Farm House (the farm run by Mr Bunce) and Jersey Farm (run by Mr Bill Booty up to the 1950s). The modern residential estate of Bunces Close is situated in this area.

Steam threshing

The top photograph on the opposite page shows a steam traction engine driving a threshing machine in front of Saddocks Farm Cottages in the 1930s. The main threshing contractors employed by Eton Wick farms were Wards of Egham and

Poulters of Burnham. The contract staff often slept rough in the farm barns. Until the advent of combine harvesters, corn was cut and tied in sheaves by binders. To protect them from the wet until they could be collected, the sheaves were stacked in 'stooks'. Stooks comprised of eight or so sheaves stood on their butts, the rounded side to the weather. Reg. H Tarrant of Crown Farm is engaged on this activity in the picture at the top of the following page, taken probably in the 1950s. The sheaves were then collected and built into ricks, often on the actual corn field, sometimes back in the farm, until the corn could be threshed and the straw baled. Skilfully built and thatched ricks were a common site in South Field along the Eton Wick Road and on the farms. The photograph below shows Reg. J A Tarrant of Saddocks Farm as a toddler c1930 in Saddocks rick yard; probably these ricks were thatched by Reg's elder brother Cyril. (The two Reg's were first cousins, sons of George and Arthur, respectively).

Farm Horses

Harry Cook ploughing with a team of horses c1920s.

Harry and and brother Alf came to Eton Wick from Henley, where they had been farmers, in the early 1920s. Harry married villager Ethel Dace. They had one daughter, Eileen. Ploughmen were very proud of the straight furrows they cut. Over the course of a day they walked many miles up and down the field, maintaining tight control of the plough handles and the horses. Harry worked for Saddocks Farm, among others. The picture below is of 'Porky' Banham tending his horses in front of the barns of Saddocks Farm c1920s.

Hay Making

This photo is early 1930s, and is probably taken on South Field, with the trees and hedge of Eton Wick Road running from the left behind the horses. Cyril Tarrant is on the cart (arms folded); the others are believed to be, from the left: A Banham (Porky), Bert Baily and Arthur Tarrant on the rake.

The horse gives way to the tractor.

This picture was taken around 1930 on Manor Farm, and could well have been taken with the historic significance of the occasion in mind, as George Tarrant and his son Bob (in white shirt) stand by their new iron wheeled Fordson tractor, about to replace the horse in the background.

The village blacksmith.

This is believed to be blacksmith Arthur Gregory (left) with Charlie Benham, which would date the photo as early 1920s, as Jack Newell became the village blacksmith in the mid-1920s. The forge was located in Wheelwrights Piece, across the common brook opposite the Greyhound public house. It was a favourite place with the village children for spending a few hours watching the blacksmith at work. The lads helped with bellowing the fire and other odd jobs, while the girls could get steel hoops made for a penny.

The hayward.

Mr 'Hammer' Stannett was for many years the Lammas hayward. He is pictured here minding cows and horses on South Field. Windsor Castle is in the left background, and the 'Chinese Bridge' and river just out of the picture on the right. The hayward grazed the cattle over Lammas lands from the commons, the Slads, Eton Wick Recreation Ground, South Field and back home. The milking herds have virtually all gone, and with them the hayward, but residents still benefit from the rural legacy of open fields all around them, as Eton and Eton Wick are virtually surrounded by Lammas or common land, preventing urban sprawl. A similar photograph of 'Hammer', has featured in a number of county and national publications. Haywards Mead housing development was named after the hayward.

The following two pictures are of harvesting in South Field, with the Eton Wick Road in the background. In the upper picture, Cyril Tarrant is reaping the corn with a binder towed by a Fordson tractor c1940s. The tractor has steel wheels (pneumatic tyres came to Eton Wick fields in the late 1940s) and ran on 'TVO' - tractor vaporising oil. The lower picture, also in South Field is c1960s. It shows a Fordson Dexter tractor driving a baler, following on behind after reaping and threshing by the combine harvester. The driver is believed to be Andy Stratton, with Ian Sainsbury walking behind.

Harvesting in South Field.

The Jacobs family

This photo is c1900 and shows the Jacobs in front of their cottage, which faced onto Dorney Common. The Jacobs worked on the nearby farms. Note the caged bird at their feet, a popular addition to many households in those days. The Jacobs were the grandparents of Lily Bye and Edie Stewart who, until they died just a few years ago, were still resident in Eton Wick.

'Haymakers at tea Eton Wick' 1894

This photograph is used by kind permission of the Leicestershire Records Office and is precisely entitled and dated by the photographer, artist George Henton. It is almost certainly taken in South Field, north of Chinese Bridge. Note the heavy boots and variety of caps and felt hats.

Milk rounds

Milk rounds were a major feature of Eton Wick farmers and smallholders. Up to the 1930s there were some 20 milk producers, ranging from owners of one or two cows to pedigree herds in Eton Wick and in the villages around its borders, and 7 or 8 delivery rounds, many of them to Eton College Houses. In the top photograph Harry Bunce sits in his milk float at the bottom of Brocas Street, probably pre-1939/40 war. Note the old fashioned churns. Roundsmen had to be particularly quick when stepping onto their floats, as their horses, knowing the rounds so well, proceeded on their way immediately they felt a change in the balance of the float shafts. It was not unknown for College boys to hold their smaller colleagues under the delivery horse's nose in the hope the horse would bite. Some of

Harry Bunce's farm is part of what is now known as Bunces Close housing estate. Harry's home was 'Rosedale', a detached house next to the old parsonage. It was said that Harry had no right of way from his farm to the Eton Wick Road, and used to drive his horse 'Kitty' and trap along the Common to Eton Wick. In times of flood, George Tarrant allowed him to drive through Crown Farm (Harry's sister Charlotte was married to George's son Alf, which presumably helped). Harry served on the Eton Wick Parish Council and several other committees. The lower photograph shows Pam Jaycock and Joan Cooley (of Little Common Farm) with their electric milk float, pictured on their final round in 1993. They were the last local operators.

Milk Round and chickens

The upper photograph shows Cyril Tarrant on the Saddocks Farm milk round c1930–32. The milk was ladled from the churns to the customers' jugs. Cousins Bob and Reg Tarrant also ran milk rounds from Manor Farm and Crown Farm, respectively. When it became compulsory to retail only milk that had been pasteurised, the milk was collected in tankers from the farms and processed by specialist dairies such as Neville & Griffin of Slough. Some farms initially brought the processed and bottled milk back to their farms and continued their own rounds. In the main it was left with the processors to retail the product. These were the post-war days of the Milk and Egg Marketing Boards. Cyril took over Saddocks Farm from his father Arthur. Besides growing feed crops for dairy and beef cattle, the farm grew cereals; pigs were kept by Arthur and chickens by Cyril.

The lower photograph, c1970s, is of Cyril and his wife Vera with his prize silver laced wyandottes. By then Cyril had retired and bred chickens for shows. He became a well known poultry judge and wrote a number of articles on specialist and rare breeds for the exhibitor magazines.

SECTION TWO

Businesses

The Old Dairy and Eton Court, Eton

The Windsor & Eton Dairies building was situated next to photographers Hills & Saunders in the High Street. It was a 15th century house with a central hall and solar wings, with many alterations over the years. After much deterioration the dairy was demolished in 1967. Many of the older residents of Eton will remember the small statue of the golden cow in the window, how cool it was to step down into the dairy on a hot summer's day, and of being served by Rosie, the auburn-haired assistant.

The lower photograph shows the entrance to Eton Court car park looking towards the High Street. Part of the Austin Leigh and Baldwin Institute is visible on the left of the photograph. What the shops that can be seen in the High Street were selling then cannot be discerned from the picture.

The 'new' shops, Eton Wick

In 1951 the Eton Urban District Council built a parade of seven shops in what had been the Brewers (Meux) Field alongside the Shepherds Hut. Before these shops the village had been supplied by mobile traders and a few individual shops scattered throughout the community, most of which were adapted homes. These traders served the village well and in many respects it was to be regretted that the new purpose built shops would in time displace the older businesses. The shops both old and new in Eton and Eton Wick at that time were service shops supplying daily essentials such as meat, fish, groceries, fruit and vegetables, and dairy, bakery and chemist products. By the end of the 20th century, this service trade was fast vanishing from the local streets, as car ownership and supermarkets became the norm. The first businesses to take up occupancy in 1951 were (from the nearest shop in the photo): Barnes (wet fish and game), Arnold's (butchers), O'Flaherty (chemist), Clinch (bakery), Darville's (grocery), Anderson (newsagent and tobacco), and Bond (greengrocery). When Doreen Tarrant (née Clinch) retired, Darvilles expanded into this unit, the wet fish shop became a fish and chip shop (now also a Chinese take-away) and the butcher's became a hairdresser's salon.

The changing face of Ada Cottages

Ada Cottages are immediately west of the Three Horseshoes public house on the Eton Wick Road. The first photograph shows the village's first Post Office and bakery shop – Lovell's General Stores. Thomas Lovell was in the stores from c1880 to c1914. Possibly Thomas Lovell is the man in the shop doorway, and his baker is standing by the delivery barrow. Brother Fred Lovell had a draper and footwear business.

In the late 1930s Ada Cottages housed the 'UNEED US' haberdashery. The two partners were Marjorie Morris and Mabel Woolhouse. Marjorie was the village Girl Guide Captain. Mabel was the Guide Lieutenant and the daughter of Ted Woolhouse, the Cycle Shop proprietor. Wartime clothes rationing made the clothes shop unviable.

Clifton House

Like many houses on this section of the Eton Wick Road, Clifton House was built on land formerly belonging to houses and smallholdings that faced on to the common (now Common Road). The Greyhound public house is at the Common Road end of the original plot, with houses (along The Walk) built in between. In 1840 the first village school stood on the site. When the present school was opened in Sheepcote Road in 1888, the building was used as the Village Institute. In 1902 Pratts of Eton and Windsor built the present building, selling paints and hardware (as advertised on their large hoarding on the wall outside, which was still legible nearly one hundred years later). From 1908 to 1913, the period when this photograph was taken, Ernie Harman ran the stores. The Post Office transferred here from Lovell's Stores about this time also. The Harmans came to Eton Wick in 1908. By then Lovell was a well established village family name, and descendants of both families are still in the village.

The shop is probably most remembered as Chantler's Grocery shop. Mr Chantler (senior) came to the Wick in 1929. His son Harry ran the shop from the time of his father's death in 1932 until he retired in 1973. It finally closed as a shop in 1986 and became entirely residential. Harry was a popular and helpful community man, serving on several village committees and always happy to make deliveries, particularly important in the days of few cars. During WWII the back of the shop was reinforced and used as the Air Raid Precaution Office for the eastern end of the village, probably because the shop had one of the four telephones in the village in the 1930s. Harry was an air raid warden, and supplied and fitted gas masks for most of the villagers. An air raid shelter was just across The Walk road, in front of Joan Taylor's shop. The last shopkeepers in Clifton House were Mr and Mrs Winters, who eventually closed the shop around 1986, and converted the building into flats. The name 'Clifton' has passed to the Senior Citizens residence, Clifton Lodge, constructed adjacent to the shop in the 1970s.

Durable advert

This sign, on the side of Clifton House, almost certainly dates back to c1904 when Pratts ran the shop. It is just readable, nearly 100 years later. It reads: General Stores, Oils, Colors, Varnish, Putty, Whitening, Size. Turps, Methylated Spirits, Ready Mixed Paints, Paper Hangings. It was used for many years as a shop hoarding with posters pasted over it. The confused lettering at the top may be due to Pratts name being changed to the next proprietors, the Harmans in 1913. Between the board and the letter box there used to be for some 60 years a ladder, for use in the event of a village fire emergency. For some of this period there was also a fire hose here.

Thames View Stores in the 1970s. John Barron, the proprietor, pictured outside, possibly just off on a delivery run. Originally one of a pair of semi-detached houses known as Wellmans Cottages it became a retail outlet in 1910 when William Hearn sold saddlery and harness, etc. After Barron's grocery stores closed it became an aquarium and pond shop, finally reverting to a private house in 1994. The opening of the new shopping parade in 1951, and later the superstores in Windsor and Slough brought about the decline of the village's small family run shops.

Bill Sibley and Moores Lane petrol pumps. Bill opened the Moores Lane filling station in 1958, converting the end house of Primrose Villas to a newsagent/confectionery shop. The row of houses comprising Primrose Villas were built for James Moore in 1885. His house, with a distinctive bay window facing onto the Alma Road side, being the one converted to the shop. During the 1930/40 period before establishing the shop, Bill sold newspapers on College Corner, Eton, and delivered papers throughout the village, from his then family home in The Walk. The petrol pumps are now dry, and the shop is owned by John Prior.

Market gardeners

The Ayres/Prior family outside 'Home Close' in Bell Lane c1910. Adults from left: James Ayres, Hannah (daughter), her husband Harry Prior (Sen.) and children Avis, Harry (Jun.) and Mary. In the 1880/90s James sold off some of his land, parcel by parcel for the building of the then designated Boveney New Town – Alma, Inkerman and Northfield Roads. He gave, free of charge, the plot on which Annie Tough and her followers built the Methodist Chapel in Alma Road. In 1953 Harry Prior Jun. sold much of the family orchard for the building of homes in Lower Bell Lane.

Shakespere Stores, Alma Road

Fred and Olive Willsher outside their shop in 1939. Olive ran the shop; Fred was a musician on a liner. In its early days the shop was in the hands of Charles Ayres; the Willshers took the shop on from Lucy and Jess Binfield in the mid-1930s and handed over to Mr and Mrs Gerry Chinnery in the mid 1940s. Note the pre-war style advertising plates on the shed door. The last business use before becoming a domestic residence was by Harry Cook, Builder/Jobber.

The George Williams ironmongery shop in the eastern half of Ada Cottages in the 1970s. The shop will be remembered by many anglers for supplying fishing tackle. George came to Eton Wick from Windsor and was a cobbler by trade. He transferred his business to the second parade of Council shops when they opened, later retiring to Australia, where he died. The school lollipop man in the white coat is Tom Cox. Tom lost a leg in WWI.

Ada Cottages and the Three Horseshoes at the end of the 20th century. Other businesses operating from Ada Cottages include Bright's Fish and Chip shop (1930s); Gurdock's Tailoring and Haberdashery (a WWII Jewish evacuee family) and Eric Springford's Shoe Repairs (1960s).

The Bonds hand over their family greengrocery business and retire after trading in the village for over 90 years. The photograph shows Bob McGrath (on the left) taking over the business from Frank Bond on July 4th 1988. Next to Frank is his sister Edith Stacey and Joan, widow of brother Albert Bond, who died in 1986. Joan ran the Bond's Eton shop. Bob McGrath formerly managed a Burnham supermarket.

Roy and Joan Arnold retired in 1998 from their Butchers shop opened in 1951 by Roy's father Ted in the then newly built parade of shops. With Roy and Joan is daughter Julie.

From the 1920s until 1961, George Mumford was the village Butcher, his shop being the left half of the house on the Eton Wick Road shown in the photograph. Until the 1960s the other half of the 'semi' was a domestic dwelling. The building has seen many uses and occupiers, including a launderette, originally set up by George Mumford, and run by his eldest daughter Betty (wife of Windsor Chief Fire Officer Fred Clatworthy). The building has also housed a car accessory shop, a florists, a bakery, and a bookmakers.

Cheers at Eton Wick

CUSTOMERS at Eton Wick's new sub office are always ready for a "whine."

But they're certainly not complaining about the service at subpostmaster Dick Harding's office. In fact they think it's the toast of the Slough area.

Because after they've collected their pensions and bought their stamps, they can browse through Mr Harding's well-stocked shelves, offering everything for the home brewer, from wine presses to corks.

"It seems we are unique," said Mr Harding, who operates the office in Bell Lane with his wife, Valerie. "Eton Wick would appear to be the first village to have a sub-office within a home brew shop."

Dick and Valerie Harding keep their customers happy by offering home brewing supplies in thei Eton Wick sub-office.

The village Sub-Post Office moved to the Bell Lane parade of shops in 1985. The Post Office was originally located in Lovell's Bakery & Stores in Ada Cottage until moving to Clifton House around the time of the Great War. Dick Harding became Eton Wick's new Postmaster. He and his wife Valerie took on one of the shops in the new parade, at first trading in hi-fi, records and electrical goods. They progressively established themselves as home brew suppliers. Dick died in retirement in Coleford, Gloucestershire.

The Blue Bus Service and proprietor Mr Bert Cole on his retirement in 1966.

Until the Blue Bus Service started around 1922, villagers walked to Windsor, and schoolboys to Eton, If they were lucky they got a lift on a horse and trap, or cart. The first bus was quite small with a bench seat each side for the passengers. This, and subsequent buses up to the 1930s, were entered by steps and handrails at the back. The service was very popular as it ran at all times and in all weather. It frequently pulled up at any point between specified bus stops to pick up or drop off passengers and always found room for everybody. Late buses after the cinemas and shops closed were often packed with as many standing passengers squeezed together as were seated. In the mid-1930s, another service known as 'The Marguerite' (cream and brown livery) plied the same routes between Windsor Castle, Eton, Eton Wick, Dorney and, less frequently, to Maidenhead. The Marguerite service only lasted a few years. Ultimately the increase in family car ownership slowly forced the successful Blue Bus Service into decline.

Among the popular drivers with the Blue Bus Service there were, as well as Bert and his son, Ted Jeffries, John North, John Bell, Bill Mitchell and Gerry Austin. Gerry is pictured standing in front of one of the Blue Buses (the man on the left) in the photograph. During WWII, Gerry drove ambulance vehicles for London Transport, often bringing wounded servicemen from the docks. After the war he drove the Blue Buses, and then worked for the council, often sporting a top hat for special occasions.

SECTION THREE

Characters and Families

The village 'Bobby'

P.C. Stanton pictured in front of his home, the village police house at the north end of Moores Lane, Eton Wick, around the turn of the 20th century. P.C. Stanton appears in another archive photograph of 1897 at the Queen Victoria Diamond Jubilee celebrations in Eton. There was a village policeman until 1976, when P.C. Tweddle retired and the Eton Police Station closed. The last time a resident policeman used this house was in 1960, by which time new police houses just off the Eton Wick Road had been built. Undoubtedly the old style village 'bobby' made it his business to observe and hear what went on in his community, and could often check crime before it became more serious or repetitive.

Alf Spayne

During the Second World War, Alf ran camps from spring to autumn at Boveney Lock. The boys mostly came from the Slough area. Alf was a keen rowing instructor and a strict disciplinarian, and by the time he had finished with them, the boys were extremely fit. He taught many hundreds to swim. In the top photograph, Alf is at the back on the right. The picture lower was taken in 1999 on the footpath to the river. Behind Alf is the Scout Hut (left) and the houses along Eton Wick Road, including Clifton House (centre).

Billy Cooley, farmer

The photograph shows Bill driving his tractor and trailer on North Field with the Windsor Relief Road in the background c1995. Bill took over Little Common Farm after the death of his father. Many will remember him and his wife Joan delivering their milk.

Bill was the only Eton Wick resident to achieve the distinction of becoming Mayor of the Royal Borough of Windsor and Maidenhead (in 1991) after serving many years as Councillor and a Justice of the Peace.

Miss U M Badger, M.B.E.

Miss Ursula Badger came to live in Eton from Wales during WWII and since that time has worked unceasingly for the townsfolk. In 1991/92 she was Mayor of the Royal Borough of Windsor and Maidenhead. Ursula was awarded the M.B.E. at Buckingham Palace on 21st December 1994.

The Charteris Day Centre, Eton

Miss Badger was the instigator of the Charteris Day Centre for the elderly. The Centre is in Eton Square, and was opened by the late Lord Charteris of Amisfield. The building was previously the Doctors' Surgery, and before that, the New Inn Public House.

Florence Ivy Wilson

Florence was the daughter of Harry Briddes, a smallholder and greengrocer in the village. As an author of plays she adapted her maiden name and penned as Ivory Brides (from a nick-name given her by a boyfriend). She was a stalwart of the Village WI, a Councillor on Eton Urban District Council, Treasurer of the Youth Club and served on many other committees. She was also a member of the Baldwins Bridge Trust, and wrote a book on the subject. She was always reliable and honest in her decisions which won her many friends. She had a daughter, Margaret, who became leader of the Youth Club girls' section, and a son Don. The photograph is c1970s.

Harry Cook and Bill Sharp

Harry (left) and Bill were both very keen gardeners and accustomed to being on the winner's rostrum. Here they are pictured as Allotment Holders Prize Winners c1970. Harry ran a small general building and decorating business from his premises in Alma Road. He was a very keen cricketer and was the regular wicket keeper for Eton Wick Cricket Club. He was also an untiring worker for the Methodist Chapel. Both men were very popular in the community.

Councillor Ronald Clibbon

Ron Clibbon cuts the ribbon on the seat presented to the village by the Eton Wick and Boveney Women's Institute to mark the Buckinghamshire Federation's 50th anniversary in 1970. The Institute members in the photograph are, from the left: Mrs Attride, Mrs Kohler, Mrs Willsher, Mrs Hessey, Miss Banister, Mrs Joan Jones, Mrs Wilson, two other people are hidden from the camera, Mr Clibbon, Mrs Wyeth, Mrs Leary and Mrs Paintin. Ron Clibbon first became a councillor with Eton Urban District Council in 1949/51, and again from 1953 until 1974 when the E.U.D.C. became the Eton Town Council. He served as a Bucks. County Councillor from 1964 until 1975, and then a Berks. County Councillor. He was Chairman of Finance from 1974 to 1977. He was also a J.P. from 1959 to 1987; a member of Berkshire Magistrates Courts Committee 1975/87, a member of Thames Valley Police Authority 1974/87 (Chairman 1977/85) and a member of the Police Council for the U.K. 1983/8. He was the Secretary and Treasurer of the Eton Wick Village Hall Committee 1964/72 and Chairman of the Royal Albert Institute Trust from 1983 to date.

Samantha Claire Whitty 1971-87

Bryan Whitty constructing the brick pillared wooden gates to the churchyard of St John the Baptist. Bryan and Vivian donated the gates in memory of Samantha, their daughter, who died at the age of fifteen. The gates were dedicated by the Rev. Colin Pontin in 1993.

John W Moore

Moores Lane is named after John Moore, who came to Boveney New Town (as it then was called) from Rotherhithe, Kent. His daughter Annie (a founder of the Alma Road Methodist Chapel) was married to Charles Tough, who became manager of Bell Farm. John Moore had Primrose Cottages and Snowdrop Villas built in Alma Road; his own house was at the end of Primrose Cottages abutting Moores Lane. Boveney had its own Council from 1894 to 1934 and Moore was the first chairman.

Mr and Mrs H. Burfoot

Mr and Mrs Henry Burfoot Jnr were active members of the community for nearly half a century. Mr Burfot was secretary of the Village Hall Management Committee, a member of the Parochial Church Council and a sidesman. Mrs Burfoot was on the committee of the Eton Wick Nursing Association and was secretary when the Infant Welfare organisation started in 1915. She was also a member of the Church Ladies' Working Party and a founder member of the Eton Wick and Boveney Women's Institute.

Mr Edward Littleton Vaughan 1851-1940

This photograph of Edward Vaughan was taken in the 1930s. 'Toddy' Vaughan was a house master in Eton College for 27 years. It was his initiative that bought Agars Plough and Dutchman's Farm for the College. In 1879 he climbed the Matterhorn, and was an enthusiastic horse rider despite sustaining a crippling leg injury in the process. He took a great interest in Eton Wick and was the village's greatest benefactor as a list of his many contributions would testify. He donated land and funds for building the Village Institute (now the Village Hall), gave generously to the Horticulture Society and the Church and its Sunday Schools. He was founder of the first scout troop in the village and its first Scout Master (he was at camp with the troop near Weymouth when the Great War was declared in August 1914). In c1907 he formed the Harriers and Rifle Club, started the Boys' Club in c1935 and was President of the Eton Wick Football Club. He also served on the Council and was at one time its Chairman.

Mrs Dorothea Vaughan

Dorothea was married to E L Vaughan (Toddy) in the mid-1920s. He was by this time in his 70s. After Mr Vaughan's death in 1940 she continued to support her husband's village interests with much generosity. She gave chairs to the Institute insisting that they be bought from her birthplace, Ireland. She donated a stained glass window to St John the Baptist Church, which was dedicated to the memory of her late husband. Although handicapped by deafness in later years she still attended Youth Club meetings as its President. Dorothea died in 1954. The Vaughans owned the Wheatbutts in Eton Wick, but lived at Willowbrook, Eton.

The Tough family

The Tough family at Bell Farm. Charles Tough was manager of Council-owned Bell Farm. This photograph, taken around 1908, shows Charles and his wife Annie (both seated, facing camera). The other adults are believed to be Annie's sister (seated right), and Archibald Chew with Charles and Annie's niece Annie F Moore standing on the left. Archie Chew and Annie Moore married in 1910, and like the Toughs, were pillars of the Methodist Church in Eton Wick.

The Tarrant family

A Robert Tarrant and family first appear on local Parish Records in the mid-1700s. The family appears to have had their roots in the west Berkshire/Hampshire/Dorset areas. This photograph, taken between 1900/05 shows seated, left to right: Robert's descendant James Tarrant, his wife Julia (nee Hawkins of Pigeon House Farm, Dorney) and George Lowman (landlord of the three Horseshoes); and standing, left to right: James's son Alf Tarrant and wife Charlotte (née Bunce) who took on Little Common Farm, Percy Holden (proprietor of a gun shop near Windsor Bridge), daughter Rosie Tarrant (a teacher at Silchester House School, Taplow), an unidentified young man, daughter Fanny (taught at Eton Wick School, married name Woolhouse) and son Arthur (then of Manor Farm). Besides acquiring four farms, James was a warden at St John the Baptist church. Missing from the photograph is his son George Tarrant (Crown Farm and father of Reg) and daughter Minnie (married name French, grandmother of the French Brothers, Windsor Boats). The photo was taken in the garden of Saddocks Farm House and is embossed 'Photographers Spearman, Eton Wick'.

The Prior family

The Priors were a well known Eton Wick family. Those in the photo, c1915/16, are, back row, left to right: Harry (Junior), Kate, Nellie; seated: Hannah (mother), Avis, Mary, and father Charlie. Charlie and Harry were life-long choirmen and served as sextons for St Johns. Harry Junior operated a greengrocery business from his horse and cart.

Neighbours at Albert Place c1940.

Dick Hood in uniform, his mother, neighbours Mrs Ethel Cook, her daughter Eileen and husband Harry. The young girl with Eileen is believed to be a London Evacuee living with the Cooks. Harry Cook was a ploughman. Dick Hood was one of twelve Eton Wick/Boveney WWII fatalities.

The Bond Brothers

The sons of Albert and Florence Bond taken in 1935. Albert started up the village greengrocery business with a donkey (and later a horse) and cart when he was about 14 years old in 1899. The family came to Eton Wick from Hazelmere, Bucks. Albert's brother Tom Bond also ran a Fruit and Vegetable growers and wholesaler business in the Wick. They were also cousins of Roland Bond (Contractors). The brothers are, from left to right at the back: Frank and Albert Jnr., and in the front, Edward and Ernest (twins) and Alfred. There were also three older sisters Edith (married name Stacey), Eva and Nora (married name Bell). Albert (junior) continued the mobile side of the business (now using mechanised transport and Frank joined the firm when they acquired the first of the village council-built shops in 1951. They subsequently added shops in Langley, Holyport and Eton.

The Dace family

Mrs Dace is standing on the door step at Harding Cottages. Her daughters Ethel (married Harry Cook) and Alice (married name Akers) are on either side of Nellie Powell. The cottages were demolished for the building of Clifton Lodge Home for Senior Citizens. It is believed the railings went as scrap metal as part of the 1939/45 War Effort.

Local men avert disaster

It was just past 4 p.m. on December 7th 1992 when Boveney Lock Keeper Dave Gibson heard a sharp crack as the mooring chains of the 150 ton hotel barge 'Actief', tied up in the weir stream, snapped. The river was running high and fast as the great 90 foot barge was swept along in the six to eight knot current. Dave Gibson immediately telephoned his District Office, alerting them to the impending danger heading towards Windsor Bridge, before cycling furiously along the partly flooded towpath to overtake the 'Actief'.

Reaching Eton, Dave joined College Boatyard staff Paul Cutler, Peter Stevens and manager John Cork (see newspaper cutting below) on board the motorised punt 'Ark' and headed upstream to intercept the oncoming barge. Fortunately for local residents, the 'Actief' had been momentarily halted, caught up on the river bank a short distance upstream of the Windsor Relief Road Bridge. Dave and John boarded the vessel and cast the fore and aft anchors. Meanwhile Senior River Navigation Inspector Phil Green, alerted by Dave's telephone call had contacted the French Brothers' Windsor Boats Office and with a team from Bray Steamers helped to complete the recovery operation. Had the 'Actief' (which can only just get into Boveney Lock) struck the Relief Road 'Queens' Bridge or Windsor Bridge the possible damage and consequent flooding would have been a major local disaster. At the 1993 Ross McWhirter Memorial Dinner in the Michelle Temple Hall London, Dave and John received the well deserved McWhirter award for their resourcefulness and bravery.

Left to right: Paul Culter, Peter Stevens and John Cork.

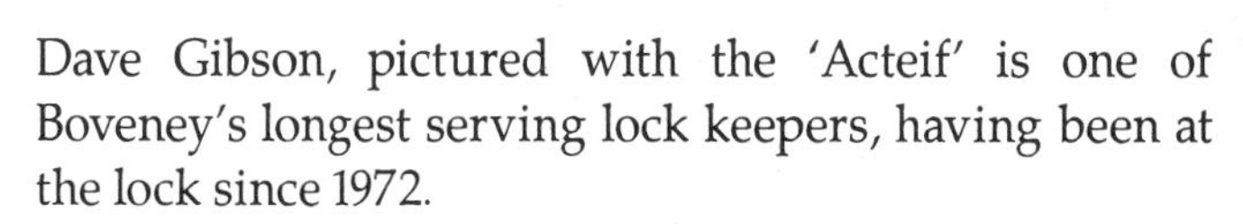

Dave Gibson, pictured with the 'Acteif' is one of Boveney's longest serving lock keepers, having been at the lock since 1972.

An Award deserved but not forthcoming

Beyond doubt the most outstanding charity work in Eton Wick was performed by Jennie Dowson and Maud Rivers. Jennie and Maud worked tirelessly from the 1960s until 1984, when ill health overtook them. An appeal for recognition, recommending the award of M.B.E. was made to Prime Minister of the day Margaret Thatcher. Regrettably no award was forthcoming, despite the recommendation being supported by the Vicar of Eton, a Doctor from the Eton Surgery and a former Chairman of Eton Urban District Council and County Councillor. Jennie died of cancer and Maud suffered a stroke before another attempt to gain recognition could be made.

The list of beneficiaries is almost endless: among the many to benefit substantially from their work were 17 village recipients and a further 18 from outside the village; also autistic children, Clifton Lodge, the Youth Club, St John's and St Gilbert's churches, a telephone for Pensioners, the Village Hall, the Scouts and Brownies, taxi fares for the sick, gifts for the elderly/deserving, etc. The gifts to individuals included a paid visit to Lourdes. There were donations to disc radios at Wexham and Heatherwood Hospitals, a kidney machine for a London Hospital, equipment for the Eton Surgery, plus some 190 incidental items such as wheelchairs and special need mattresses, etc. to hospitals.

Jennie lived all her life in the same house in Hope Cottages, Common Road. Her father, Jack Newell was the village blacksmith from about 1922 to the 1940s. The photograph taken in the 1960s shows from left, Jennie, Maud and Jennie's grandson Lawrence Dowson salvaging a cart wheel from the smaller of the two ponds situated between Wheatbutts Cottage and Dairy Farm, no doubt hoping to sell it for charity.

J T Ireland

At one time the village firm of J T Ireland employed around 60 men and apprentices. James (Jimmy) Ireland started his business on leaving the army after the Second World War, and built extensively in Eton Wick and Dorney. Eton Wick developments include east side of Tilstone Avenue and the eastern end of Queens Road. In this photograph Jimmy is presenting a gold watch to Charlie Simpson to mark his 25 years service with the company. Mrs Ireland is on the right. Jimmy was a great supporter and benefactor of the village Scouts and the Youth Club. He became an Eton Urban District Councillor in 1947 and served as Chairman of the Housing Committee, and then as Chairman of the Council up to 1954. Between 1952 and 1981 he served on Buckinghamshire County Council as Chairman of Works, Planning, Staff and Finance and also as Vice Chairman of the County Council for 10 years, besides various other appointments. In 1957 he became a Magistrate and served as Chairman for 15 years. In 1975 he became Deputy Lieutenant of Buckinghamshire and in 1982 was appointed Commander of the British Empire (C.B.E.).

George Batt, Verger

In 1993, to mark 60 years of faithful service to the village and St John's Church, George received a certificate from Neville Thorman, secretary of the Churchyard Fund Committee. George has served as choirboy and choirman, Sidesman, Church Warden, and has held the post of Verger for many years. The occasion was the 20th anniversary of the Churchyard Fund Committee.

George Paget and Chris Rigden

George used his horse and cart to trade in greengroceries, removals and other odd jobs. He also ran pony and trap trips for tourists, operating from the Windsor Castle taxi rank. George and his horse-drawn transport appeared in several films, which included the 'Carry on' series. George served in the Western Desert Army during the Second World War.

Chris owned the Cockpit Restaurant in Eton High Street before taking over the Barksfield Bakery in Dorney. In the 1960s Chris regularly waited each night at the Burning Bush bus stop for the last Green Line coach of the evening, bringing his stepdaughter Penny home from her leading role in the 'Black and White Minstrels' show at London's Victoria Palace Theatre.

The photograph, taken in the late 1940s shows the now removed Eton Parish Church spire, the Roman Catholic Church and the 'Well's' timber built shed, now replaced with an office block.

The Hoods

Brothers Albert and Dick Hood delivering coal to the Three Horseshoes public house. Also in this c1935 photo are younger brother Don Hood (on the running board) and the landlord's son Peter Short. Within a few years, Dick was to become a WW2 fatality in Italy. The brothers had taken over the business from their father, Scottie Hood. The business converted to mechanical transport around 1932, when a fire at the Sheepcote Road stables killed the horse and destroyed the cart.

Bravery Medal for Wolf Cub William Hodge

Chief Scout Robert Baden Powell awarded the Gilt Cross and Certificate to nine year old William Hodge of the 1st Eton Group on April 17th 1929. While playing on an ice covered stream in South Meadow, Eton, on the 1st March 1929 Alan Kingston (6) fell through the ice. William and another eight year old boy tried to pull him out, but the ice broke under their weight and they went under also. William continued his efforts alone after his eight year old colleague left the scene, and he finally managed to pull Alan out, averting a probable fatality.

BE PREPARED

This Certificate

is Granted to Wolf Cub William Hodge of the 1st Eton Group as evidence that I have awarded him the Gilt Cross in recognition of the pluck & promptitude he displayed in the rescue of a boy who had fallen through the ice at South Meadow, Eton, on March 1st 1929.

Dated April 17th 1929

Robert Baden Powell

Chief Scout

The upper photograph shows the Certificate with Baden Powell's signature, and the lower photograph is of William (on the right), with Alan.

Harry Chantler

Harry Chantler and his wife Hilda being presented with a cheque and a bound book containing the signatures of many local residents marking their respect and affection, on the occasion of Harry's retirement in March 1973. Harry's father took on the village store at Clifton House in 1929. Following his father's death in 1932, Harry carried on the grocery business and sub-post office for over 40 years. He was active in many local organisations, being a member of Eton Poor Estate, the Parochial Church Council and serving as a School Governor. The presentation took place at the Women's Institute meeting and was made by the president, Mrs Joan Ballhatchet (right).

Henry Babington Smith Plaque 1983

The Vice Provost of Eton College and a Trustee of the Village Hall, Mr David Macindoe, unveils a plaque dedicating the new boundary wall of the Hall to the memory of Henry Babington Smith, who was for twenty years a much loved Trustee and benefactor of the Village Hall. Pictured with Mr Macindoe are Eton Town Councillor Mike Tierney (left) and Village Hall Chairman Jim Burger, and on the right, Henry's brother, Mr Bernard Babington Smith. Following his retirement as a master at Eton College, Henry Babington Smith served the village community in many ways until his death in 1982. During the 1960s he voluntarily kept the churchyard tidy and the grass cut. Only when the task became too great was a committee established to find ways of funding the maintenance. Henry Babington Smith served on this committee too, until his death. The central bed of shrubs in the churchyard is also dedicated to his memory.

The Hammertons

The Hammerton family at a village cricket match around 1909. Mr Hammerton stands behind his three daughters, and seated at the right-hand end are believed to be his sons George, Fred and Charles. The Cricket Club was founded in 1889 and played for many years on Eton Wick Great Common. This photograph was taken at the west end of the common near Sheepcote Road.

Village Youths c1913/14

This picture was probably taken in Inkerman Road and is one of the few photographs in the History Group's records with no definitive information. Most, if not all the youngsters would have served in the Great War. Tentative identifications suggest that the second from left, back row is Fred Hammerton (see family photo above) awarded the M.M.; third from the left is Ern Brown (killed at Passchendaele in 1917); the single lad in the cloth cap, standing is Norman Lane (R.F.C.); the sailor on the left is Roll Bond, and the one on the right Bill Wicks, both of whom saw service at sea with the Royal Navy.

SECTION FOUR

Churches and Schools

Eton Wick Church of England School

This photograph was taken c1950s and shows the oldest part of the school, built in 1888. The old farm track leading past the school entrance became known as Sheepcote Road. An earlier school had existed, built in 1840 on part of the Greyhound public house plot, which then extended to the Eton Wick Road where Clifton House now stands. Larger school premises were needed when Boveney New Town was developed in the 1880s, resulting in the Sheepcote Road development. Further expansion was not necessary until c1950 following the rapid development of the village after the Second World War, and then again in 1965. In the early 1900s, the school was for infants and girls to the age of 14. Boys between 7 and 14 years attended Eton Porny School. In 1940 Eton Wick School took in infants and juniors, boys and girls between 5 and 11 years. Pupils over 11 attended the secondary school in Ragstone Road Chalvey, Slough (opened in 1939) and those gaining scholarships went to grammar and high schools. The longest serving teacher was Miss F. Stearn (1903–1935), who was also Head Mistress.

Eton Wick First School. The Classes of 1995.

St John the Baptist Church and School, Eton Wick

The village church was constructed in 1866 and consecrated the following year. It was designed for a congregation of 180 worshippers and built on former Crown land given by Queen Victoria, along with £100 towards the cost. It was Eton Wick's first purpose built church. There is some evidence of preaching and services held in farm buildings and other sites before the church was built. The school buildings can be seen on either side of the church. The 1888 part of the school is on the left and the 20th century classrooms on the right. Both church and school were built in the corner of Sheepcote Field. In 1851, between the use of farm buildings for services and the building of St John the Baptist Church, the former school, built in 1840 approximately on the site of Clifton House (The Walk) was licensed for Divine Services for a period of some 15 years.

St Gilbert's Roman Catholic Church

In 1954 Father Dunstan encouraged local Roman Catholics to strive to finance the construction of their own church in Eton Wick. At that time Sunday morning Mass was celebrated in the Village Hall (for which the hire charge was 4 shillings). Ten years later, in 1964, on the day before Palm Sunday, the Church of St Gilbert was blessed by Bishop Parker, assisted by the Prior and Chapter from the community of Cannons Regular at Datchet. The land on which the Church stands, on a corner of the former allotments near the Village Hall, was purchased for £1500; construction costs were £16,000. This photograph was taken in 1998.

Boveney Church

This photograph of the church came from the family album of the late Arthur Tarrant. It is thus probable that the seated lady, front left, is his wife, Bertha Ellen (née Gregory), who came from Kensington as an orphan in 1910 to live and work with her relatives, the Harmans, in their village store at Clifton House. This would also give the approximate date of the photograph.

The portrait photograph is George Selwyn, curate of Boveney Church in the 1830s. George Selwyn was educated at Eton College and Cambridge (for whom he rowed). He returned to Eton to teach, which is when he served as curate to Boveney before moving on to Windsor. In 1841 the Archbishop of Canterbury appointed him as the first Bishop of New Zealand, where he served with distinction for 26 years before being recalled to England to become Bishop of Lichfield for the last 10 years of his life. He was, in fact, the first and the last Bishop of New Zealand, as the country was subsequently divided into a number of dioceses each with its own bishop. He went far after his Boveney curacy.

Boveney Church

The correct title for the church is 'The Chapel of St Mary Magdalene' It is a small building measuring approximately 51 x 19 feet. The bell turret at the west end of the chapel has two bells by Ellis Knight dated 1631 and 1636, and a third, probably 16th century. It stands 30 yards from the river bank about two miles west of Eton on a site that has been a place of worship since before the Norman conquest. The building origins are obscure, but was first mentioned in 1266. Until 1911 when Boveney liberty was ecclesiastically annexed to Eton, St Mary Magdalene was a chapel of ease within the parish of Burnham. An Act of Parliament in 1737 to make Boveney a separate living failed for want of sufficient endowment. In 1892 a temporary arrangement was made whereby the Vicar of Eton undertook the spiritual care of the people of Boveney and in that year extensive restoration took place, the work being executed by Henry Burfoot & Son of Eton Wick. The church was declared redundant in 1975 and there was a possibility that it would be demolished or sold for conversion to residential use. Local residents, however, fought to save the chapel and it was eventually leased at a peppercorn rent to a London Charity Group known as 'The Friends of Friendless Churches' who now maintain the building. It is still a consecrated church building and is used at least three times a year at the Patronal Festival of St Mary Magdalene in July, and at Harvest and Christmas Festivals.

There are contradictions associated with this quaint little chapel of just 13 bench seats, each for 4 persons and themselves estimated to be some 500 years old. A book written in the 19th century states that the writer was surrounded by the graves at Boveney Church. Many enquiries to date have failed to reveal any burials having been made there. Another popular claim is of the building having been a chapel for bargees; again no evidence and doubtful. The village of Boveney was certainly large enough to warrant a church in those early years as it compares with many other villages that had churches. As an off shoot of Burnham Abbey it was regarded by the nuns as a Liberty Chapel, free to some extent of the rigid order of the Abbey. (Some of the above information was extracted from the *Victoria History of the Counties of England*, edited by William Page F.S.A. and published by the St Catherine Press in 1925).

New oak fence for St John the Baptist Church Yard in 1920.

Volunteers, several of them ex-servicemen, building an oak fence alongside the un-kerbed Eton Wick Road. Among the group from the left are: 1st: Mr Hyde, 3rd: Mr Percy, 5th: Walter Woolhouse; 2nd from curate Mr Tarrant, 1st man with spade is Mr Haverly, 2nd with spade Mr Bert Benham.

Arthur Hood, gardener at St John the Baptist Church.

Arthur has enthusiastically kept the churchyard tidy for many years since a maintenance scheme started in 1972. This photograph was taken in 1997. The community is proud of the standard of upkeep achieved, believing the churchyard is among the tidiest and most peaceful in the district.

St John the Baptist Church Choir 1922/3. The boy standing on the left unknown; Harry Prior in suit; Bill Harman; Rev. Onslow; Hugh Haverly. Centre row: unknown; Joe Sibley; Ron Lane; John Lane; Charlie Prior (sexton); Maurice Lane; Harry Johnson. Front: Mr Baker Choirmaster; next three unidentified; Harry Pearce; next two unidentified; G Prior. The St John the Baptist Choir kept going until the 1950s. The choirboys' 'pay' in the 1930s for a weekly choir practice and two Sunday Services was between 2/6d and 3/6d (12½p to 17½p), depending on age and ability.

St John the Baptist Church Choir outing c1919/20. Very few of the trippers have been identified. Hugh Haverly is leaning on the centre passenger door. Harry Prior (Junior) is by the handle of the front door (no hat). Bill Harman is seated at the back wearing a light coloured jacket. Harry Johnson in the cap is seated front second row next to Harry Prior. Harry Nason (Choirmaster) is next to Hugh Haverly. The bus has solid tyres, a 12 mph speed limit and a Slough telephone number '215'. Each row of seats has its own door.

The Methodist Chapel

The Chapel is in Alma Road, in the left immediate foreground. When first built Alma Road was in Boveney New Town. This old photograph is believed to have been taken around the turn of the 19th century (note the tricycle and lack of a footpath) The houses, Primrose Villas, were developed by John Moore in 1885. Moore's own house is the one at the far end of the row, beyond which is farmland.

The Methodist Chapel, Primrose Villas and Alma Road at the turn of the 20th century. Beyond what was John Moore's house is now Moores Lane and the 'new houses' built in the 1950s.

Eton Wick School

A photograph taken between 1903 and 1906. At this time the older boys attended Eton Porny School. Very few have been identified. The teacher is believed to be Miss Stern, the Head Teacher; the young sailor boy is probably Charlie Hammerton, who lost his life in the Great War. Third from the left of Miss Stern is possibly Amy Hammerton. On the left in the back row is Edith Stacey, daughter of the Shepherds Hut landlord.

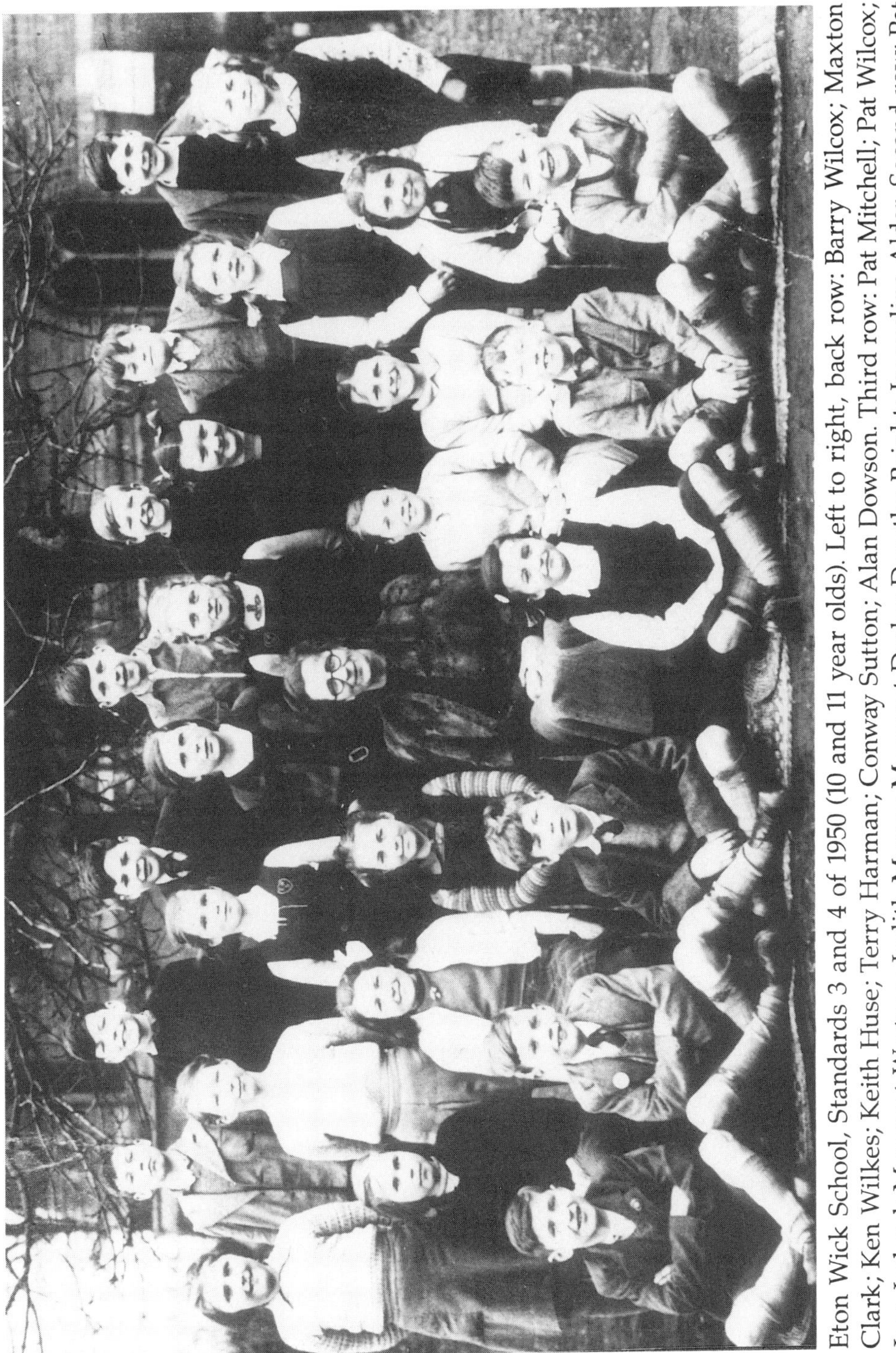

Eton Wick School, Standards 3 and 4 of 1950 (10 and 11 year olds). Left to right, back row: Barry Wilcox; Maxton Clark; Ken Wilkes; Keith Huse; Terry Harman; Conway Sutton; Alan Dowson. Third row: Pat Mitchell; Pat Wilcox; Jean Ireland; Margaret Western; Judith Mayne; Margaret Drake; Dorothy Bright; Jacqueline Alder. Second row: Pat Day; Fay Kirby; Gillian North; Miss Ida Rooke, Head Mistress; Sylvia Robertson; Kathleen Johnson; Daphne Johnson. Front row: Tom Foster; Les Hood; Alec Benham; Daphne Cooley; Roger Wilcox; Tony Johnson.

Eton Wick Play group 1978

The Play group ran from 1967 to 1991 and enrolled a total of 564 children during the 24 years. The adults officiating (back row, left to right) are: Pat Emery, Viv Whitty, Margaret Everitt and Mary Morrell. The children are (back row): Teresa Woodley, Rory Whyte, Debbie Boyd, Debbie Steptoe, Clair Low, Daniel Pitcher, Mark Wheeler, Kirsten Reeves, Daniel Lloyd and James Woodisse. In the front row: Jeremy Butteriss, Sharon Hance, Julie Ansell, Andrew Murray, Trudie Holmes, Sandi Blackman, Tracy Mills and Philip Riddle.

Eton Porny School

Although there is some duplication in the following two photographs taken in 1934 and 1935, together they include representatives of many well known Eton and Eton Wick family names. This photograph was taken in 1934. Back row: George Clark; Chris Stevens; Eddie Mann; George Batt; Ted Munday; Murrey Clarke; Peter Short; Stanley Lipscombe. Third row: Wally Nuth; George Moss; Roy Morris; unidentified; Aubrey Paice; Alf Turner; Norman Carpenter; Arthur Keith Second row: unidentified; Don Cull; Peter Dugan; Douglas Cullum; Jim Chamberlain; Alf Bampton; Frank Hester; Doug Sharp; Alec Donaldson. Front row: Maurice North; Gordon Cullum; Doug Stagge; Maurice Young; Frank Bond; George Newell; David Shepherd; unidentified.

Porny Senior Boys, 1935. Back row: Murrey Clarke; George Batt; Alf Bampton; Maurice Benham; Maurice Young; Chris Stevens; Frank Hester; Bob Mumford. Third row: Peter Short; Maurice Smith; ?. Bryant; George Moss; Bob Huse; Roy Morris; Les Hamblin; Dave Shepherd. Second row: Aubrey Paice; George Clarke; Ron Charlton; Arthur Keith; Peter Dugan; Maurice North; unidentified; Mick Lynch. Front row: Roger Josie; Eric Golding; Alec Donaldson; Les Laurence; unidentified; Stanley Lipscombe; Ted Munday.

Eton Porny Girls School, c1932. Back row: Ena Haverly; Dorothy Perkins; unknown; Isabel Knott; Dorothy Goodall. Third row: Nina Birch; Gwen Allen; Irene Vickery; Peggy Elkins; Eileen Houson; Margaret Essan; Mary Dewar; Phyllis Talbot. Second row: Vera Snell; Kathy Quarterman; Jean Morris; Joyce Neighbour; Muriel Goodall; Bessie Weeks. Front row: Bessie Beasley; Margaret Lawrence; Winnie Thorn; Clara Herbert.

Eton Porny School. The first Porny school was built in 1812 for boys and girls born in wedlock, funded by monies left by Mark Antony Porny, a French emigre, in gratitude for the asylum given to him. He taught French at Eton College and was an authority on Heraldry. In later life he became a Poor Knight at Windsor Castle and after his death on the 2nd May 1802 he was buried in the precincts of the Castle. The first school was situated behind Nos. 29 and 29a High Street, Eton. These were the houses of the Headmaster and Headmistress, the actual school rooms being reached through a stone-flagged passage. In 1863 the Porny School moved to its present site in the High Street (lower photograph) and the old school became the Parish Room for entertainments, meetings, etc. Since World War I it has been Eton Ex-servicemen's Club (top photo).

St John the Evangelist, Eton

The foundation stone was laid on October 21st 1852 by Prince Albert. Originally built with a spire, the church was completed in 1854. When the spire became unsafe it was replaced with a tower in 1953. Due to dwindling congregations, the church became redundant and was acquired by Eton College, who effected major modifications. Now, the new church is located on the first floor, accessed via a spiral staircase and a lift. The local Doctors' surgery, and the College Sanatorium are on the ground floor. The top floor provides residential accommodation. The lower photo was taken from South Meadow in 1999, and the upper picture from the High Street, probably in the early 1900s. It is certainly pre-1922 as the stone pillars have since borne two bronze Memorial Plaques commemorating 93 men from the parish who gave their lives in the Great War.

SECTION FIVE

Community Organisations and Social Life

Eton Wick Over 60's Club

The picture was taken on a Club outing on the Thames to Hampton Court in 1987. The Club is very popular, with a good varied programme, and meets weekly at the village Football and Social Club premises. On the left aboard the riverboat is the then club organiser, Eric Springford. The organisers seeing the Club into the 21st century are Sheila Jarrett and Pam Jaycock.

This photograph was taken on an outing to Mapledurham c1979. From left to right: Olive Willshire, Jim Kinns, Reg Moore, Renee Thompson (organiser), Rose Cooley, Gladys Moore, and Joyce Kinns. The lady on the right has not been identified.

Village organisations and social life

Many organised groups and clubs have flourished in both Eton and Eton Wick over the years, with activities such as sport, youth organisations, amateur dramatics, Womens Institutes, Whist Drives, etc. all represented, one of the most recent being the Village History Group. The fact that these organisations have been supported is a credit to the residents, as Eton and Eton Wick have not had large populations, and organisations and clubs need members. In the 1750s, there were only fifteen dwellings in Eton Wick, rising to twenty-two by 1797. These were in the north east part of the village as we now know it. The numbers gradually rose during the 19th century. In 1861, 450 inhabitants are on record, growing to 520 in 1881, then Boveney New Town was incorporated, doubling the 'Eton Wick' population.

There are no written records of the formation/demise of most of the groups, and only limited photographic records of the members or their activities. Some groups of course pre-date photography. The earliest recorded groups were Mutual Help Groups; some of today's older residents may still remember the pre-State Welfare era when the early demise of a village resident prompted a door to door collection to help the surviving dependants.

The known clubs and societies of Eton Wick and Boveney are listed overleaf with approximate dates of their existence. The listing is not necessarily complete. Many of the groups owe their initial existence to Mr E L Vaughan (1851–1940) who gave financial help to many organisations and most importantly gave the land and the Institute building (now the Village Hall) where most activities took place. 'Toddy' Vaughan was the first village scout master and founded the Boys' Club in the 1930s (among others).

1826	Eton Excelsior Rowing Club (written records exist dated 1826)
1811–c1830	The Three Horseshoes Friendly Society
Early 20th century	The Village Institute Slate Club (All four Eton Wick pubs had 'slate' clubs at some time)
1879–c1940	Eton Wick Horticultural Society
1940–current	Allotment Holders Association (successor to Horticultural Society)
1885–early 19th C.	Church of England Temperance Society
c1880/90	Fife and Drum Band
c1840	Providence Club
1890–1904, c1906–? and 1934–37	Boys' Clubs
1889–1966	The Cricket Club
1900–1902	Church Lads Brigade (Village)
c1903	Night School
c1907	Rifle Club
c1907	Harriers Club
1912–16 and	Boy Scouts
1926–current	Boy Scouts (re-formed)
1927–current	Girl Guides
1902–1950	Mothers' Union
1907 and post-WWI	Black and White Minstrels
c1890–c1910	Working Men's Club
c1910–c1960	Village Hall and Vaughan Club
c1925–1998	Whist Club (Women's Recreation Club)
c1900–current	Sisterhood (Methodist Chapel)
1933–current	Women's Institute
c1930s	Tilstone Tennis Club
c1907 and 1946–52	Athletic Football Club and Boys' Minor Football Club
1952	Athletic Football Club amalgamated with Eton Wick Football Club
Current	Football and Social Club
1946–current	Mixed Boys' and Girls' Youth Club
c1940s–current	Parent and Teachers' Association
Current	Castle United Football Club (Sunday League)
Current	Bowls Club
c1960–current	Ladies Club (Methodist Chapel)
1920s–current	Cubs
1920s	Brownies 1st Pack
1950s–current	Brownies 2nd Pack
?	Beavers
1940s	Young Wives Group

1940s–current	Over 60s Club
1940s	St John Ambulance
?	Methodist Youth Club
?	Church of England Youth Club
1948–51	Unity Players Concert Party
1962–71	Shoe String Concert Party
1992	The Village History Group

Eton Urban District Council

This is a photograph taken at the social gathering marking the end of the Eton Urban District Council in 1974. Between 1894 and 1934, Eton Wick and Boveney had their own Parish Councils, each of five members. These Parish Councils joined with Eton in 1934 to become the Eton Urban District Council. After another forty years in 1974, they all became part of the new Royal Borough of Windsor and Maidenhead Council which comprises fifty-nine members, the Eton wing being represented by just two. The new Eton Town Council decision-making powers and authority was to be much restricted.

Eton Wick Village Hall celebrates the Millennium

The Rev. Paul Reynolds unveils artist Tim Harvey's painting of St John the Baptist Church in the Village Hall, on the 4th of January 2000. Tim is the Art Master to a series of adult classes held regularly in the Hall.

The Village Hall Committee also generously commissioned commemorative mugs, giving them to village children under the age of 14 years and to adults over 65.

Some of the recipients of the commemorative mugs are pictured here on 2nd January 2000. From the left they are Brenda Irvin, Eva Bond and Edie Stacey. Those issuing the mugs are Margaret Everitt, Joan Neighbour and Zena Hunt.

Eton Wick Horticultural Society Show

The Society's first show was in 1878 and it became an annual event held in the Wheatbutts Orchard during August. There were competition classes for vegetables, flowers, fruits; classes for children's card mounted grasses, floral designs and gardens of wild flower heads and seeds. The social attractions included a beer tent, a band, dancing, and fairground rides and side shows. The Society also took part in the Windsor Hospital Parade held in September of each year with a horse and cart float grandly decorated with members' produce which was afterwards donated to the hospital. The Society did not survive WWII, although its successor, The Allotment Holders Association continued to hold smaller events. This photograph is believed to have been taken in the early 1900s. No names are known.

The Horticultural Society's float, c1931, decorated with donated produce and about to leave Common Road to join the procession of decorated floats, Fire Brigades, musicians, etc. taking part in the King Edward VII Hospital Parade. The route took the procession to Slough, Eton, up Thames Street hill and on to the Hospital. The horse and cart was traditionally supplied by Bert Bond, the village greengrocer. Parades ceased after WWII when the National Health Service funded the hospitals. On the float is Ted Bond. Standing, left to right, are Mr Benham, George Paget, Bert Bond, Mr Hemmings (Secretary) Joe Clark, Hugh Haverly, Ern Woolhouse, Bert Benham (not believed to be related to the Benham on the left) and Harry Young.

Eton Wick Cycling Friends

Photograph taken c1900. Left to right: Nobby Talbot, Edward Hammerton, George Kirby, Arthur Woolhouse, Alf Miles and Jack White. The photograph was taken in Burnham Beeches.

The Eton Wick Minors Football Club

The photograph is of the Club's 1948 outing to Margate. In the back row left to right is the Windsorian driver (name unknown), then Harry Wakefield (secretary), Frank Bond and Harry Pearce (committee members), Des Russell, Mrs Pearce, 'Chub' Bennett, Mrs Wakefield, Dennis Phillips, Bill Ingram, Mrs Hall, Ann Bright, Ray Haverly, Sheila Robertson and Sheila Spiers, ?, and Cecil Thorn (committee member). In the front are Alan Smith, 'Cooie' Barton, Mike Thorn, Bob Snaichel, Peter Frost, Phil Harding, John Newport, Eileen Bolton, Vic Merkett and Ray Mumford. The two young girls on the left are unidentified, the two on the right are Monica Pearce and Julie Wakefield.

Eton Wick Youth Club

Many of the village's former teenagers from the 1950s onwards will have happy memories of their days as members of the Youth Club. The club also attracted members from surrounding towns and villages. Quite a number of members in fact went on to marry their fellow club members. In this picture, Frank Bond, club leader from 1950 to 1961 and chairman for many years after that, receives a presentation to mark his retirement as chairman from Chris Foreman and Val Chamberlain (to become future married partners). In the centre is Mike Newlands, former leader and new chairman. To the right of Frank is Patron and former chairman Jim Ireland and club member turned leader, Geoff Low.

Eton Wick Youth Club Camp, St Ives 1958. For many years the Youth Club held an annual two week summer camp in Cornwall. The club worked hard to raise funds to buy camping equipment. In these days the cost to the members varied according to age and was typically (rail and coach fares inclusive) from £8 for 15 year olds, rising to £16 for 18 year olds and adult helpers. The campers are at the back, left to right: Des Russell, Frank Bond, Mick Phillips, Andy Lewis, Terry Harman, Les Hood, John Jeffries, Don Middleton, Cecil Thorn, and George Lund. In the centre row: Tony Clibbon, Ron Branwhite, 'Mo' (Maurice) Nicholls, Jacquie Hodge, Val Bailey, Norah Sumner, Joyce Russell, Margaret Wilson, Tony Johnson and Conway Sutton. In the front: Geoff Pardoe, Richard Jordan, Tony Gallop, Terry O'Flaherty and Ian Lewis.

There are six leaders or former leaders of Eton Wick Youth Club in this photograph, taken c1987 at a reunion when former club members, ex-leader and marriage partners Richard and Carol (née Chamberlain) Jordan returned from New Zealand for a holiday. After being a club member in the 1950s, Richard took on the leadership of the club and later became a full time youth worker at the Hook, Chessington Youth Club before emigrating to New Zealand in the 1970s where he initially continued with his full time youth work. From left to right are Frank Bond, Richard and Carol, Mike Newland, John Lovell, Geoff Low and on the right, the then current leader, by this time paid and appointed by the County.

The Youth Club organised and sponsored many activities including sport, canoe building and an annual Club Camp in Cornwall, as well as fund raising events such as the 'Wicko' Carnival and helping out villagers by cutting logs for their winter fires. In this picture the 'Crusaders' skiffle group perform on the village hall stage for fellow club members in 1958. The 'Crusaders' went on to be a highly regarded local group, and were voted 'best group' at the skiffle competition held at the Slough Adelphi cinema. Indeed a 'demo' tape was submitted to BBC radio, but turned down as 'they sounded to much like Lonnie Donegan'. In the photograph are Peter Hennessey, Andy Lewis (tea chest base), Tony Clibbon, Tony Francis (guitar and vocalist), Paul O'Flaherty (wash board), Terry O'Flaherty (drums) and Mike Knight. Some group members and their successors are still performing at functions.

Eton Wick Youth Club members cutting logs for the aged in 1956. Sawing logs: Geoff Pardoe, Mike Knight, and sitting on the timber is John Alder. The axeman is Bill Critchell.

KEEPING THE HOME FIRES BURNING

By courtesy of "Windsor, Slough & Eton Express"

DURING the winter week-ends the members of Eton Youth Club, near Windsor, have done a good job for needy villagers. They have sawn up and delivered 11,000 logs to over a hundred local families so that they could be sure of having a

All this has meant a great deal of personal effort week after week. But it's been well worth while, for the club has received a huge bundle of "thank you" letters from grateful people. The work was organized by Mr

From 1955, club boys chopped logs and delivered them to the aged. In 1956 alone over 11,000 logs were delivered. Trees available for logging were notified to the club by the Council and Eton College. Club girls supplied the loggers with refreshments. For its services the club was awarded the Hospital Saturday Fund Cup, received a written commendation from the Buckinghamshire County Council Chief Education Officer and was featured in the National Boys Clubs press (see picture). The Club age range at the time was 14 to 21 years. By the end of the 20th century, the age range had reduced considerably, partly by the introduction of a junior club in the 1960s, and partly as a reflections of nationwide social changes.

Eton Wick Youth Club Camp 1962 In the back row from the left: Derek Harrison, Ray Emery, Ted Turner*, John Stacey, John Betterton, Richard Jordan, Les Emery, Arthur Gittens, John Newell, Ian Wilson*. John Lee*, unidentified*. Centre row Peter Tarrant, unidentified, Colin Harrison, Barry Alder, John Alder, Fraser Hatch, John Durbin, Jim Alder, Frank Ormond, Willy Welford, unidentified*, unidentified*, John Gittens, Frank Bond, Mick Bell. Seated in the front: Nancy Sharp, Christine Drewett, Susan Miller, Carol Cullum, Caroline Miller, Susan Jordan, Jennifer Paintin, Margaret Wilson, Joyce and Des Russell with their son Ian.

The photograph opposite was taken at the popular club camp site on John and Kitty Roger's 'Hellesveor' Farm, St Ives, Cornwall. Although only four years after the 1958 club camp photograph shown elsewhere, there is virtually a new 'generation' of members. Those marked with an asterisk * are members of Denham Youth Club, who joined in several annual camps as for a time, Frank Bond was also the Club Leader at Denham. A few years after this photo, Derek Harrison with his family ran a restaurant and fish and chip bar at the sea front in nearby Perranporth; elder brother Colin emigrated to South Africa. Eton Wickers may remember Ian Wilson and Ted Turner (Denham members), Ian worked in the Bond's greengrocery shop in Eton Wick, subsequently becoming manager of one of their other shops; Ted became owner of KBG Engineering in Alma Road. Richard Jordan and sister Susan emigrated to New Zealand, and John Gittens to Canada. Christine Drewett and Les Emery, John Betterton and Nancy Sharp, and Colin Harrison and Margaret Wilson (daughter of Councillor Ivy Wilson, no relation to Ian Wilson) subsequently became partners in marriage. It is noticeable how many Eton and Eton Wick family names of the 19th century are still represented in this 1962 photograph.

Eton Girl Guides Camp

The summer camp was run by Mrs Grizel Hartley, wife of Eton College master, with Miss Margery Mead. Photo taken about 1937. Left to right: Betty Devonshire, Betty Morris, Hilda Irvin, Edith Weeks, Gwen Allen (on running board), three unknowns, Winnie Thorn, Lilian Branwhite, Eileen Horsgood, Everlyn Irvin and Jean Morris.

Eton Wick St John Ambulance Brigade

Members Ann Harding and Derek Smart receive awards in 1968.

Eton Wick and Boveney Scouts

Left to right: David Springford, Peter Lines and Tony Cutts receive their Queens Scout Badges in 1955/6.

Eton Wick Scout Camp, Osmington Mills near Weymouth August 1914. Left to right in the picture: Bill Woolhouse, George Percy, Bill Bond, Scout Master E L Vaughan, C Jacobs, Ernie Weatherhead, Ern Thomas, C Balm, and George Newell.

The camp was held at the outbreak of the Great War; George Percy was destined to be killed serving on the Western Front, and Bill Woolhouse to became a P.O.W. He suffered severe facial wounds, which were tended to by his captors. Scout Master Mr Vaughan was then tenant at the Wheatbutts (which he later purchased and leased out), and devoted himself to the services of Eton Wick.

Eton Wick and Boveney Scout Fete c1950s. The Scouts held their annual fetes in Wheatbutts Field and later in the recreation ground to raise funds for a new scout hut and other activities. On the left is the Rev. David Evans, Parish Vicar. Fourth from the right is Mrs Ireland, then Mr J T Ireland, Mr Fred Bond (fete treasurer), and Mr Bob Bond, Scout President In front of them are the winners of the children's fancy dress competition.

Eton Wick and Boveney Scouts 1933. At the back: Stan Bond and George Bright. Fourth row from the front: unidentified, Jack Ling, Ern Lovell, Bob Cook, Bryant. Third row: Stan Bright, Ern Lynch, Basil Bavin, Ken Weller, Bob Huse, unidentified, Jim Stannett, Gordon Paintin, George Newell, Francis Holcombe. Second Row: Frank Bond, Fred Sibley, Cyril Short, Ernie Coke, unidentified, Miss Clatworthy (Akela) Peter Cooley, Harold Woodley. Front: Arthur Hood, Sid Gomm, Dick Harding, Ken Lovell, Doug Slade, Ed Bond, Fred Harris, Ern Bond, Alf Turner, Walter Pates, Albe Bond, Jim Newell and Maurice Young. This particular Scout Troop was formed in 1926. The Assistant Leader of an earlier troop, Frank Church, was reported killed in action in 1916 on the Somme; a few years later in WWII, Stan Bond was killed in the Desert campaign and Walter Pates (an air gunner) over France.

Eton Town Scouts learning their knots c1930s. The scouts are receiving their instructions from Fire Officers Fred Husted and Reg Mead. Eton College also had their own strong group of scouts pre-World War II, based in a well kitted H.Q. hut just off Judy's Passage.

Eton Wick and Boveney Scout Camp, Scout Rally, Beaconsfield, 1954. Mike Thorn, Alec Benham, Chris Smith (at back), David Springford, unidentified, (?) Pitcher, Rob (?) Hood, (?) Emery, Terry Harman, Tom Foster and Tony Clibbon. Kneeling on the right is Ern Coke the Scout Leader.

Ern Coke (on the left), now promoted to Group Scout Master, congratulates his son John on winning the Queens Scout Badge. Stan Humphries the village Scout Leader looks on. John later succeeded Stan as the Eton Wick and Boveney Troop Leader. Some may remember Stan as the Eton Urban Environmental Health Officer.

Opening of the rebuilt Scout H.Q. in 1998. Eton Wick Scouts hut moved from Wheatbutts' Field in the 1960s to a purpose built hut on the south side of Haywards Mead, largely due to the benevolence of Jim Ireland. In complete contrast to the generosity of Mr Ireland, the building suffered an arson attack. It was however rebuilt and this photograph shows the occasion of the opening of the new building by former England Rugby Captain Will Carling. In the back row (Cub leaders and Beavers): Helma Everle, Stephen Winspear, Margaret Dempsey, Amanda Ross, Will Carling, Christine Moran, and Akela Val Ross. On the left back row of Cubs, from the left are: Jack Farmer, Charlie Whitaker, Nivraj Jasser, Hem Singh and Mathew Towsend. In front are: Luke Fogarty, Daniel Squire, Lewis Smith, Rowan Gilbey and Peter Edwards. On the right back row of cubs and scouts are: Mathew Hunt, David Riches, Guy Dollimore (?), Nicholas Dollimore, Anthony Moran, Oliver Tyson. The beavers in front (in the light jerseys) are: Jamie Gifford, Lawrence Olney, Lewis Fogarty, James Green, Christopher Cannon and Robert Maisey, plus five beavers not identified.

Gang Show c1960. Eton Wick and Boveney Scouts, Guides, Cubs and Brownies pictured at the finale of their Gang Show. At that time they were probably still using their H/Q. Hut in Wheatbutts Field.

Eton Wick and Boveney Women's Institute

The Eton Wick and Boveney Women's Institute was founded in December 1933, due largely, like many other village organisations, to the influence of Edward Littleton Vaughan. His wife Dorothea was the Institute's first President. The Women's Institute is a national educational charity and Mr Vaughan was an enthusiastic supporter of education for the working class.

Through the years Eton Wick and Boveney W.I. has gained a high reputation for its friendliness and standard of work in the many County and National competitions and events in which it has taken part. The Institute has made its voice heard on many local issues including the closure of Windsor Bridge, the proposed closure of the Library and, most recently, the construction of the Thames Flood Alleviation Channel.

The Institute hosts events, both informative and purely entertaining for its members. To mark its 50th and 60th anniversaries in 1983 and 1993, Art and Craft exhibitions, open to all the village were organised. In 1983 members produced a Pictorial History of the village. The original is held in Eton College and a reference copy is available in Eton Wick Library.

Photograph taken on the Institute's 40th Anniversary party in 1973. In the back row, left to right: Unidentified, Mrs Greenwold, Mrs Paintin, Mrs Swatton, Mrs Harrison and Mrs Wyeth. Third row (standing behind table): Mrs Durbin (later Leary), Mrs Crook, Mrs Flint, Mrs Butler, Mrs Attride, Mrs Day, Mrs Tatham, Mrs Hessey, Mrs Harding, Mrs Ballhatchet (President), Mrs Kinross, Mrs Neate, Mrs Lund, Mrs Sharrat, Mrs Wilson, Mrs Joan Bond and Mrs Charlton (later Moss). Second row (either side of table): Mrs Millis, Mrs Elsie Bond, Mrs Friend, Mrs Jacobs (Past President), Mrs Borrett, Miss Bannister, Mrs Beckett, Mrs Jones and Mrs Ash. Front row (seated): Mrs Cutler, Nurse Lee, Mrs Wickens (Past President), Mrs Hartley (Past President), Mrs Pat James and Mrs Cooley.

The Eton Wick Methodist Sisterhood

This photograph was taken c1960. Back row (heads only visible): Mrs Slaymaker, Mrs Gardner, Miss Majorie Morris, Mrs Lily Jacobs (probably) Third row: Mrs Sophie Chamberlain, Mrs Jacobs, Miss Mary Ayres, Mrs Brown, unidentified Second row: Mrs Harris, Mrs Woodley, Mrs Paice, unidentified. The child is believed to be A. Higgins, grandson of Mrs Woodley. Front row: Mrs G Kelly, Mrs Dobson.

This interesting old photograph is a mystery, leaving much to be guessed at. It is possibly an Empire Day gathering, some time between 1906 and 1910. The location, with the railway viaduct in the background is certainly at, or near to the south side of Eton Recreation Ground. The new Recreation Ground at that time would probably not have had the benefit of hedges, as it was all formerly Lammas land.

The assembly of presumably Eton Porny school children and absence of uniformed boy scouts suggests it predates the Scout movement of 1908 (or 1910, if the formation of the Eton troop is allowed for). The flags, adults and speaker leads one to believe it was an Empire Day Assembly, a national celebration day inaugurated in 1902, May 24th to commemorate the birthday of the late Queen Victoria.

The Eton Players

The Eton Players drama group was formed in the 1960s by Mrs Alice Burrow. The group presented a number of plays, performed in the Eton Church Hall and the Parish Church. Most of the costumes were designed and assembled by Mrs Peggy Payne of Eton High Street and local jumble sales provided the materials. In the photograph, from left to right are: Pauline Evans (wife of David A N Evans, Vicar of Eton), Sylvia Collier, Brenda Herriot (wife of the Headmaster of Porny School), Ivy Bowyer, Mary Pyke, Rita Pidgeon and Barbara Herriot. The play was 'The Six Wives of Calais'.

Eton Parish Church Fete

This photograph is believed to be the 'celebrity' opening of the summer c1974 Fete, by the Emperor 'Iedo Kung Fu' and his entourage. From the left are: the Rev. Christopher Johnson, Rita Pidgeon, Lesley Ballard, Celia Russell and George Paget. George was a very well known character, often to be seen with his carriage and horses taking tourists and bridal parties to their destinations (and the odd appearance in 1960s cinema films).

The Choir of St John the Evangelist Church, Eton

Eton and Eton Wick had choirs until the 1970s. This is Eton's large and enthusiastic choir of 1966/7, pictured in front of St John the Evangelist, Eton, at that time the Parish Church. In the back row (adults): W Stickley, R Boxall, D Pidgeon, A Welsh, P Harris, R Bowyer, R Pike, J Stacey, S Fairbain, M Newland, L Pike, E Gater, C Blake, and the Choirmaster/Organist. In the middle row (boys): S Amor, R Hillyer, K Pallett, (?) Middlemas, the Rev. David A N Evans, P Angell, S Maw, (?) Maw, P Burt, W Pike. The front row: N Fairburn, (?) Middlemas, (?) Maw.

Eton Women's Fellowship

The Eton Women's Fellowship was founded in 1963 after the Mothers' Union disbanded. It meets weekly at the Eton Church Hall and as well as Eton residents, attracts members from Eton Wick, Windsor and Slough. Social events include talks, quizzes, outings and parties. This is a photograph taken at their Easter Bonnet Competition in 1998. Standing left to right are: Mrs Day, Mrs Weeks, Mrs Mummery, Mrs Bell, Mrs Brades, Mrs Bolton, unidentified, Miss Hill, Mrs Batt, Mrs E. Edwards, Mrs Cook, unidentified, Mrs Leary, Mrs Butler, Mrs Pratt. Those seated are: Mrs Bowyer, Mrs Pidgeon and Mrs Golding.

Eton Wick 'Unity Players'

The photograph was taken at the finale of the 'Unity Players' first pantomime in 1948, 'Alladin'. The Players went on to produce 'Cinderella' (1950), 'Dick Whittington' (1951) and 'Spring Parade' (1950 and 1951). The shows were written by Fred Wiggett and Tommy Neighbour. As was the case in those somewhat austere post war years, the local communities, boosted by their restless ex-service personnel put a great deal of effort into raising funds for improving local amenities such as schools, and leisure facilities for both adults and youth, and had fun in the process. The proceeds of the 'Unity Players' sell out productions went to the purchase of new kit for the Football Club. Those identified in the photograph are: Fred Wiggett (with the boater on the right), Tommy Neighbour (half concealed, 4th from the right), John Cox (5th from the right), Zena Hunt (7th from right), Eva Bond (with bouquet), Francis Alder (left of Eva), and Joan Neighbour (5th from left).

The 'Shoestrings'

The Eton Wick Variety Group were reformed in 1962 as the 'Shoestrings' to raise funds for the Village Hall extension. They staged variety shows annually until 1971, some of them skits on contemporary T.V. shows, including 'That Was the Wick That Was', 'Christmas Crackers' (1964), 'Licence to Laugh' (1965), 'Through the Rainbow' (in 1966, with ex Victoria Palace Black and White Minstrels Penny Rigden and Alan Hollidge), 'Summer Interlude' (1967), 'It's here' (1970) and finally 'Starella Fantasy' in 1971. The group performed in many venues. Comedy sketches were written by Albert Bond, Sid Eyre and Sid Gomm.

In this picture from 'Through the Rainbow' in 1966 are, back row, left to right: Kay Thompson, Sandra Ling, Rene Thompson, Sandra Wells, Jacquie Tickle (daughter of Francis in the photo on the opposite page), and Caryl Cullum. In the middle are Jane Harper and Gail Groves. In the front: Susan Bond, Leslie Chadd, Jillian Bowyer and Denise Fogarty.

Eton Wick F.C. 1929

When the club was formed in 1881, home matches were played on Dorney Common, much later moving to their present home on Eton Wick Recreation Ground.

This photo of 1929 shows the team at the front of the Village Institute (now Village Hall) long before the entrance stairs to the upper floor were covered. In the back row, left to right: Jess Binfield (committee member), Bert Percy, Tim Morrell, Bob Bond, Les Binfield, Archie Bryant, Bert Harman, unidentified, Ern Bryant. In the front row: M Porter (committee member) George Giles, Ted Watson, Bill Swabey (captain), Maurice Lane, (?) Prior, Tom Morrell.

Eton Victoria F.C. ('Eton Vics') 1933

This well known local football club played their home games on Eton Recreation Ground. In the back row from the left: Bert Cox, Ted Smith, Bill Swain, Bob Quayle, Alf Young, and Alf Flint. In the centre row: Tom Hart, Alf Haskins, Les Hall, Les Balchin, Bill Weymouth, George Birch, Harry Bampton, Stan Cutts and Doug Martin. The front row: Bill Folker, Ernie Alder, Gordon Cox, Jim Middleton, Ron Cox, Ron Martin and Albe Alder.

Eton Wick Minors F.C. 1948

The Minors were formed in 1946 following the end of the War, when Harry Wakefield and Doug Cooper formed an Under 18's village football club. They played their home games in Eton Recreation Ground. Sports kit was still virtually unobtainable due to wartime clothing rationing, so the boys played in any light coloured/near to white shirt, and Mrs Bill Sibley (mother of two of the team) made black shorts for the team from off-coupon wartime blackout material. Village colours were traditionally amber and black, but here was born the origin of black and white for the boys team. In 1948 the team were able to have this photo taken in newly bought kit. They are, in the back row: Doug Cooper, Frank Bond (committee), Jim McDougall, Alan Herd, Ray Haverly, Tony Rodwell, Harry Wakefield and Cecil Thorn (committee). In the centre row: Ray Knight, John Grant, John Batt (captain), Dennis Phillips and John Knott. Bob Horton and John Newport are in the front row. John Grant went on to play in senior league football. In later life he opened bakers shops in Windsor and Eton Wick.

Eton Wick F.C. 1953

The Eton Wick Minors F.C. changed its name to Eton Wick Athletic when it formed a senior team from former players in 1949/50. In 1952 the two village clubs Eton Wick United and Eton Wick Athletic amalgamated, becoming the Eton Wick F.C. Success was instant and the merged club won the much coveted Slough Town Senior Cup for the first time. They have won the cup again a number of times since. Captain Jack Ling is holding the cup aloft in this photograph. The team is, from left to right: 'Tich' Keen, John Batt, Mick Sibley, 'Rolly' Woodley, John Grant, Jack Ling, Ron Carter, John Sheehan, Alf Vickers and Ron Pitcher.

Eton Church Lads Brigade

This photograph was taken c1928/30. The Eton Company of the Church Lads Brigade is assembled and ready to march off to the High Street to join the long parade of floats, fire brigades, and bands taking part in The Windsor Hospital Parade. The parade was held annually to collect funds for the hospital before the post war days of the N.H.S. The Church Lads Brigade was a fine and disciplined outlet for youths. It is believed that the Eton Company was formed in 1899. Between 1900 and 1902 attempts were made to raise an Eton Wick Company without success. The Sgt. Major in the photo is Bill Morris. The drummers in the front row are: Ernie Alder, unidentified, Albe Haverly, and Sgt. (?) Alder. The trumpeter is Tom Forman, George Birch has the big drum and the man with the medals is Fred Bosher.

Eton Fire Brigade c1920s

The Eton Fire Brigade was manned by local volunteers, most of them traders. The 'Merryweather' fire engine in the picture was named 'Princess Alice', and was 'christened' by Princess Alice in 1913, when it replaced the horse drawn pumps. The 'Princess Alice' can still be seen in the Vintage Vehicle Museum at Caister Castle, Great Yarmouth. Eton has not had its own brigade since WWII. In the front row of firemen 4th from the left is Fire Chief Fred Husted, and 2nd from left is James Dugan. James (Eton baker) had been the driver up to 1910; he then became chief engineer and driver and in later years the Brigade Chief Officer. His son (also James) served as a fireman before the 1939/45 conflict.

Eton Wick Cricket Club

The Cricket Club was founded c1889 and played in its early seasons on the Great Common. After the 1914/18 War, home fixtures were played on Saddocks Farm, where the rural outfield attracted several regular visiting teams.

The photograph was taken on the occasion of the Club winning the District Cup in 1931. In the back row: Norman Lane, Harry Cook, John Lane, unidentified, Ted Moss. Centre row: unidentified, Ern Bryant, Sid Harman, (?) Percy, Arch Bryant, Fred Hammerton, Jack Stacey, Frank Lane, Hugh Haverly, and umpire Mr Henry. In the front: the first two on the left are unidentified, Tich Prior, Bill Moss, Edwin Buckland, Ted Morris and resident farmer, Arthur Tarrant. Saddocks Farm House is in the background.

Leading the team in is Doug Tarrant, in sequence behind him are his brother Reg (sons of Arthur), George Lewis (Clerk to Eton Town Council), Doug Slade, Jack Stacey, Stan Allaway, Stan Hewett, Ian Lewis (George's son) and Bert Prior. The photograph was taken in the mid-1950s; the club closed down in the 1960s.

SECTION SIX

Highdays and Holidays

One for you dear reader. This group is pictured in the churchyard of St John the Baptist (west end of the church on the right) and behind them, the original (1888) part of Eton Wick School. The old toilet block, now gone, is to the right. The questions are, when was it taken, what was the occasion and do you recognise anybody? There are some family likenesses, and some clues. The trimmed tree and the sound fence suggests perhaps early 1920s. If it was post 1932, identification would have been possible by comparison with other known photographs. It is possibly a Sunday School group as boys only attended Eton Wick School up to the age of seven. They are all too well wrapped up for it to have been a summer outing. We welcome your suggestions.

The Duke of Edinburgh opens the Stockdales Road Recreation Ground, October 14th 1952. The Duke, escorted by Jim Ireland, local builder and Chairman of the Eton Urban District Council, unveils the Plaque commemorating the opening. The much older existing recreation ground (by Eton Wick Village Hall) and the Eton Town Recreation Ground were established using money paid by the Great Western Railway in the 1890s as compensation for the railway viaduct constructed on Lammas ground in 1849.

The newly built Stockdales Road flats overlook the dais as Council Chairman Jim Ireland makes his speech welcoming the Duke of Edinburgh. On the left-hand end of the dais is Councillor Bert Wolfe, Mrs Ireland, Clerk to the Eton Council George Lewis (white shirt and tie) and Mayor Jennings of Slough. Mr McKinnon, Bursar of Eton College stands behind the Duke, and the Deputy Chief Constable is on the Duke's left.

'Wicko' Carnivals

The biggest one day functions ever held in Eton Wick were beyond doubt the 'Wicko' Carnivals, held in the recreation ground on summer Bank Holidays between 1967 and 1981. The Carnivals offered fairground rides, various stalls, and arena events which included tug-of-war (attracting teams from the Midlands and across Southern England), re-enacted battles by the Southern Skirmishers, lady wrestlers, steel bands, go-carts, fancy dress, and 'It's a Knockout' competitions. The carnivals were initially run by the Youth Club to raise funds for the building of a games hall, and later as a joint venture with the Football and Social Club who needed funds for their own club premises. The 'Wicko' Carnivals grew from strength to strength, and by the end were attracting over 10,000 visitors on each occasion. It finally outgrew itself, there being too few workers to maintain the standard achieved.

In the top picture, taken in the 1970s, the 'Piano Bashing' competition is nearing a conclusion. The lower picture gives an indication of the crowds that attended. Also, in this photograph the newly completed games hall can be seen (to the right of the tree, top right-hand side).

Above, the Blue Bonnets Pipe Band from London play at the 1974 Wicko Carnival.

Left, Susan Lund is crowned as the 1969 Miss Youth Club by Billy Walker, the British Heavyweight Boxing Champion. Eleven youth organisations had competitors in the Beauty Queen competition. Billy Walker officially opened the Carnival on this occasion, and the new Club Sports Hall.

The ladies compete in the 'Pushball' event in a 1970s Wicko Carnival.

SECTION SEVEN

Public Houses and Outings

The Shepherds Hut

For many years the 'Hut' was well known for having a strong darts team. The team above, pictured with their trophies in 1947/8 are, from the left: George Mumford (village butcher), J Dalby, 'Joby' Milton (father of Pam Jaycock, pictured elsewhere in the book), Walter Stacey (Team Captain), George Giles, Wally Gregory (later to become landlord of the Grapes), Les Lovegrove, Albert Hood and Fred Millis.

A Shepherds Hut outing in the mid-1950s. The 'Hut' outings to the coast had a reputation for the generous dry and wet refreshments that were provided. Those enjoying the traditional stop en route are, front row from left to right: Walt Woolhouse, Albert Hood, Dennis Robson, Spike Robson (father), Landlord Bill Colbourne; Jim Marshall (Dorney Court Farm Ploughman) is between Spike and Bill, and on the extreme right is John North (Blue Bus driver); the man on the right wearing a top hat has not been identified. Bill Colbourne was landlord from 1932 to around 1960.

An earlier (1912) Shepherds Hut group. At the back: Ted Hammerton, George Kirby and Jack Try. Second row: Jack Wilson, A Woolhouse, Jack Binfield, M Keen, Fred Pert, Fred Wilson (no relation to Jack), the man in the cap with a pipe is not identified, 'Pony' Moore and G Attride. Front row: Fred Stacey, Mr Hammerton (Sen.), Bill Stacey and Mr Porter. (Fred and Bill Stacey were the landlord's sons and Mr Hammerton their great uncle).

Jack Try, following his 1914/18 War service discharge founded the Windsorian Coach Company. Fred Pert became the organising secretary of the newly formed Boys' Five a Side Football Competition for the sons of Discharged Sailors and Soldiers.

The Shepherds Hut, c1920. The Staceys were landlords from 1899 to 1932. William Stacey died in November 1918. His widow kept the pub for a further fourteen years. Daughter Jennie Stacey, (later Harman) is in this photo. William Colbourne took over from Mrs Stacey. The pub became a Meux house, then Friary Meux, Ind Coope and, now, Fullers.

Shepherds Hut Field, adjoining the pub belonged to the brewers, and was rented out for work horses. A Pelhams Funfair was held in it annually. In 1951 the Council built the parade of seven shops, followed some time later by the Princes Close housing development. A small portion of the field remains at the back of the pub.

The Stacey family. Left to right, starting at the back: Edith (daughter), Bill (son), Roger, Bill (father), Walter, Nora, Mrs Stacey (landlady from 1918 to 1932 following her husband's death), Jennie and Fred. During the same period, another Stacey widow, with her son Jack, ran the Grapes (now the Pickwick).

The Greyhound

The Greyhound is situated at the Common Road end of The Walk. The landlords, Mrs Newell and her husband, pose outside. They took on the pub in the 1930s. Bill died in 1947 and his widow continued the business until her retirement.

The Greyhound was first licensed as a beer house in 1842. A full licence to sell spirits also did not come until over 100 years later. It is said that the pub name derived from the fact that in the mid-19th century, a former landlord's son, James Deverill, trained greyhounds. Originally, the pub garden extended right up to what is now the Eton Wick Road; the track that ran along side the garden was known as 'Deverill's Walk'. Much later, the track became a road with houses either side, now called simply 'The Walk'. The pub's former working stables are a popular skittle alley.

An outing from the Greyhound. Outings to the coast or to race meetings were annual events for pubs, clubs and works from the 1920s until car ownership became the norm in the 1960s. Many trips were undertaken on the village Blue Buses, not exactly as comfortable as today's coaches. Of historical note, the village blacksmith's forge was located behind the trees that can be seen on the right of the photograph. Those embarking on this outing from the Greyhound pub forecourt c1938 are from the left: Mr Mitchell, the next man is unidentified, Harry Caley (in the flat cap), 'Son' Emery, Bill Stannett, Ernie Benham, Bob Slaymaker, Bill Brown, Harry Turner, Bill Pardoe, Jack Benham, Joe Newell, George Paget, Bert Young, Charlie Benham, Tom Cox, Bill Newell (landlord), Bert Benham, Alf Hester, Charlie Phipps, Ern Miles (postman) and Fred Nappin. In the front: the pub lodger 'Curlie', Tom Race, unknown, Charlie Stevens and George Newell.

Mrs 'Lil' Newell

Lil Newell ran the Greyhound pub from the 1930s, initially with her husband Bill, and then continued on her own after his death in 1947 until her retirement in the late 1960s, becoming perhaps the longest serving publican in the village's history. This photograph dates to the 1960s. Lil passed away c1984.

Bill Colbourne

Bill became landlord of the Shepherds Hut in 1932 and kept a very popular house for approximately the next 25 years. Here he is pictured drawing free pints for the pub's day trippers to the coast. 'Jock' Lockhart is behind Bill with a glass of beer in his hand. Jock was an ex-Scots Guardsman, married to local girl Grace Harman, and worked for builders J T Ireland as a carpenter.

The Willow Tree Public House, Eton

No details or names are known for this picture, but the button holes, polished boots, boaters and waistcoats suggest sometime between 1910 and 1925, and they were possibly going to the races. The Willow Tree closed as a public house in October 1975, the last landlord being Mr Jack Foster. In the 1950s Eton Wick Minors football team used the bar on Saturdays as a changing room, their home games being played on Eton Recreation Ground.

A Three Horseshoes pub outing

The outing took place about the 1930s, probably to the races. From the left: Bob Tarrant, the next two are unidentified, the driver in peaked cap, Bill Parrot, Vic Short, the landlord (with pipe), Roll Bond, unidentified, George Mumford, Frank Skelton, Harry Briddes (at the back), Jack Saunders, unknown, John North, unknown, Ern (Toby) North, unknown, Ted Marriner, (open shirt) unknown, Walter Woolhouse, (trilby hat) unknown, unknown, 'Son' Barnett, George Cox, and Mr Hislop.

This photograph is also a parade of many of the village business men. Roll Bond was the father figure of the R Bond & Sons contracting business. Harry Briddes operated a mobile greengrocery, and had stables and pig sties down what is now the east side of Tilstone Avenue. Jack Saunders was Harry's pig man. Harry sold his land to a young carpenter, Jim Ireland, just returned from WWII service who developed Tilstone Avenue on it. Ted Marriner was master baker to Barksfield of Dorney. Bill Parrot was one of the Wick's coal merchants. His stables are now the Greyhound skittle alley. George Mumford was the village butcher and Bob Tarrant ran a milk round from Manor Farm.

SECTION EIGHT

Then and Now: Comparisons

Eton Wick Village Hall

The Village Hall as it was between 1930 and 1962. This artist's impression from old snapshots is by Eric Evans. The original building, then known as 'The Institute', was opened on January 22nd 1907 and comprised the east wing only (left side of the picture). There was a billiard room and reading room on the ground floor. The large room upstairs was also used as gymnasium. The Hall was built by Henry Burfoot & Son, the local builders and given to the villages of Eton Wick and Boveney New Town by Eton House Master Edward Littleton Vaughan to promote fellowship and 'wholesome recreation' among the men and boys of the community. Very soon, however, it was open to all. In 1934 Mr Vaughan conveyed the Hall to Trustees as a Village Hall and Club. It became a registered charity, run by a Management Committee of local people. The Hall was used as the Infant Welfare Clinic from 1915. During WWII, gas masks were distributed from there, and an emergency food store and a class room for London Evacuees was established. Until the mid-1960s, school dinners were served there. For over thirty years the ground floor has been leased to the Municiple Authority for use as a Library and Youth Club.

Common Road looking east

Common Road pond and old houses c1920 (upper photo). The large elm tree in the middle distance is at the the junction between Common Road and Sheepcote Road. The Greyhound pub and Thatch Cottage are this side of it. This, the north end of Sheepcote Road, was then a gated farm track with a stile. The bottom photo, taken in the 1990s, shows the pond area infilled and grassed, and the modern Albert Place dwellings in place of the old cottages.

Common Road looking west

The top photograph of Common Road with the pond was taken in the late 1930s. The Wheatbutts is on the left. The 'old' Scout Hut in Wheatbutts Field can just be seen behind the elm trees, and beyond them, Bell Farm Cottages (now Bellsfield Court flats). A noted occupant of the Wheatbutts was film star the late David Niven, then a wartime Captain in the Highland Infantry. The ponds were used for fishing, bath tub punting, model boat sailing and skating. Note the 'young' oak tree (planted in Jubilee Year 1897), and in front of it a mound of ashes from one of the regular November the 5th bonfires. The railings protecting the tree went as part of the WWII recycling effort. The lower photograph was taken in the 1990s. The ponds were infilled in 1969.

Eton Wick Road

This section of the Eton Wick Road was formerly called Tilstone Lane. The pictures are taken from near the present day Tilstone Avenue (behind the camera and leading off to the right) looking towards Eton. The entrance to Victoria Road is on the right between the cyclist and the pedestrian on the old post card view (taken c1920) and by the cars on the modern photograph (mid-1990s).

Burfoots' 'Red House'

The 'Red House' (above) was built in 1904 in Tilstone Lane (now No. 41 Eton Wick Road) by Henry Burfoot for his son (also named Henry). In the 1870s Henry Burfoot was a bricklayer living in a small cottage by Little Common. Within 10 years he had built himself a showhouse with a yard and substantial workshops in Alma Road. He was more than a jobbing builder, advertising himself in 1891 as 'Builder and Contractor, bakers' oven builder (a speciality), hot range and boiler fixing'. His son carried on the business for the next 50 years. On his retirement he sold the property and business to Prowtings. Seven years later they sold it to J T Ireland. The J T Ireland business operated from the Red House. The business is now owned by Stephen Bond (grandson of Roland Bond), who, in the late 1990s doubled the size of the 'Red House' incorporating two shops, as can be seen in the photograph below, taken in 1997/8.

The Old Coach House, Hogarth Road (now Victoria Road)

Originally, this building served as a coach house and stable for Mr Nottage, who with a partner farmed at Dairy Farm. He lived at No. 61 Eton Wick Road, and the coach house was at the bottom of the garden. During the 1939/45 War the coach house was lent rent free (but not rate free) as an auxiliary fire sub-station. The upper photo is believed to date to the 1970s. The lower picture shows it after conversion to a home for Bill Livesey. The road was named 'Hogarth' at the end of the 19th century after the architect Hogarth who designed the terraced houses and layout of Victoria Road for the land owner, Sir Charles Dayrell Palmer of Dorney.

Shakespere Stores, Alma Road

The store was not a purpose built shop, but an adaptation of a sitting room in an end of a terrace house, dating back to the 1880s. It was for many years the main shop in Boveney New Town until the Co-op Stores arrived. Successive owners included Ayres, Binfield, Willsher, and Chinnery. It became a workshop for Harry Cook when shop trading ceased a few years after the arrival of the Council Shop Parades. Following its final demise as a business premises, the property reverted to a dwelling place, this time as flats, as depicted on the lower photograph.

Alma Road, Boveney New Town, looking west

In the upper photo (early 20th century) the terraced houses were Bell Cottages, which pre-dated other dwellings in that road. The gentleman posing in front of Bell Cottages is believed to be James Ayres, who purchased the land which later became Alma, Northfield and Inkerman Roads. He sold it off in 'parcels' in the 1880s for building. The development was known as Boveney New Town, later to become part of Eton Wick. The modern photograph shows the northern end of Bellsfield Court in the early 1990s.

Bell Lane

Bell Farm Cottages, Bell Lane, now replaced by Bellsfield Court. When this picture was taken c1950, the cottages, built in the 19th century for farm workers, were in the process of being vacated pending demolition. Bell Lane was the boundary between Eton Wick and Boveney New Town. It has been claimed that the boundary actually passed through Bell Farm Cottages, which together with Bell Cottages in Alma Road and the Shepherds Hut public house were the only dwellings west of the boundary until Boveney New Town was developed in the 1880s.

Bell Lane in the 1990s, showing the flats of Bellsfield Court, and on the right the houses of Alma Road are just visible. Bellsfield Court and other dwellings in Eton Wick became home to former long-established Eton residents, who were moved out of their cottages by housing developments in Eton.

Bell Lane (from Eton Wick Road) 1912/13. Like much of Eton Wick at that time, Bell Lane was lined with great elm trees. This photograph was one of a series of post cards. On the left is Daisy Croxford with Millie Brown on the right, both of whom lived in Boveney New Town. Until 1934 this lane was the boundary line between Eton Wick and Boveney New Town.

Bell Lane in the 1990s. This photo was taken from the same spot. The flats of Bellsfield Court are on the left, and just out of the photo, the Wick's second parade of shops. The new houses on Wheatbutts Field are behind the hedge on the right. Plans to build a library to the left of the photo did not come to fruition.

The 'Prefabs'

The urgent need for homes after World War II produced the asbestos 'prefabs'. Eton Wick's prefabs were located to the east of Vaughan Gardens and lasted until the 1960s, to be replaced by the Bell Lane shops. The cooling towers of Slough Trading Estate, where many Eton Wickers have worked, can be seen on the horizon. The photographs were taken in the mid-1960s and mid-1990s. The houses on the left of the photographs are part of Vaughan Gardens, built in 1939 and named after Edward Littleton Vaughan, the great village benefactor. In the later photo, the backs of the Bell Lane Council-built shops can be seen on the right.

Each of the views on this page are two photographs joined together and re-photographed in 'panoramic' style. The top picture is a wider view of the 'prefabs' shown on the previous page. They were built as three rows of four dwellings in Bell Farm Field. Expected to last for 10 years, they in fact stood for 20. In this 1960s picture, demolition has just started. The houses right of centre in the background, along Alma Road, are now mostly gone to make room for the flats of Bellsfield Court. The white house, centre background was Perseverence Place, built as a home and business premises for Howell, Builder c1886. In 1929 it became home and the 'Uxbridge Gas Depot' to Mr A N Harding. For some years after WWII, it was a Doctors Surgery, associated with the Sheet Street, Windsor Surgery.

The lower joined pair of photos are of Victoria Place and Thatch Cottage. The photograph can be dated by the age of the little girl in the photograph, standing with her mother Sylvia. She is Yvonne Wilson, granddaughter of Mrs Florence Scarborough who then lived at No. 21 Common Road. Albert Place flats now stand on the site. Thatch Cottage saw varied usage including as a smallholding with cows, pigs and chickens, Mrs Langridge's laundry in the early part of the 20th century, a kitchen and sweet shop run by Mrs Lane in the early 1930s and finally a home and smallholding to Mr Pass, the Lammas hayward from the mid-1930s. Reputedly, in the mid-1880s, it was the home of Mr Deverill, son of the nearby Greyhound public house landlord. The buildings faced out onto Common Road, overlooking the common pond, the mortuary, the blacksmiths and the track that led to the Isolation Hospital. Many older villagers considered this stretch of the village, from Wheatbutts Field in the west to Sheepcote in the east, to be the heart of the community.

Eton Wick Road looking west

Two comparative photographs of the Eton Wick Road looking towards Dorney Common, one taken in the early 1930s and the other in 1997. In the later photograph (bottom), St Gilbert RC Church now stands on former allotments, and further along the road there is the shopping parade between the Village Hall and the Shepherds Hut.

Eton Wick Road looking east

Another two comparative photographs of the Eton Wick Road, this time looking east towards Eton. The upper photograph dates to the early 1900s, indicated by (a) there is no shop front to Welman's Cottage, (b) the flag pole in front of Ada Cottage appeared between 1899 and 1910, and (c) the tree in front of the Three Horseshoes pub died between 1910 and 1920. The allotments on the right have been replaced by Haywards Mead and St Gilbert RC Church, as can be seen in the lower photograph taken after the installation in 1994 of the unpopular traffic chicanes.

Football

Above: A game of football in progress in the 'old' Recreation Ground, taken in the late 1940s. The houses of Haywards Mead and St Gilbert Church now block the view to the Eton Wick Road. The recreation ground was bought for the village for a sum believed to be around £400, being compensation for Lammas land lost to the construction of the G.W.R. railway viaduct.

Below: The winners in the 1999 Boys' Five a Side Competition. This traditional and popular annual event started in the early 1920s for the sons, aged between 8 and 15 years, of discharged Sailors and Soldiers of Eton Wick, Dorney and Boveney. Teams were drawn up from the entrants list, each team comprising boys from all age groups, the 14+ year olds usually being the team captains. The best and worst footballers could find themselves in the same team. The competition was traditionally held on Easter Monday with between eight and fourteen teams playing. A silver cup was presented to the winning team and their names were engraved on it. Each winning team member received a silver medal with a gold insert; runners up got a plain silver medal. After the final game, all the children lined up to receive a bun and an orange. When the number of sons of ex-servicemen declined in post-war years, the competition was opened up to all boys of the three villages who were within the age limits. In recent years the Competition rules, the date, residential qualifications, and awards, etc. have changed, not all in keeping with the original traditions, but at least an annual Boys' Five a Side Competition is still enthusiastically maintained.

Wheatbutts Field

Wheatbutts Field cleared for housing development c1980 in a photograph taken from Eton Wick Road. The 'Common Road' road sign can be distinguished, and across the field, Bellsfield Court. The old Scout Hut was located in the opposite corner from the road sign. Annual Scout Fetes were held in Wheatbutts Field in the 1950s, and the annual Horticultural Society shows from around 1878 to 1939.

New houses on Wheatbutts Field in 1990s. On the right at the corner of the road is Wheatbutts House. During the late 1920s and 1930s Mr Watson, then resident of Wheatbutts Cottage ran a small farm from here. A small thatched cottage occupied by the village nurse used to stand approximately adjacent to the estate agent's sign. Both properties were let by E L Vaughan. The field originally had some six large elm trees on each of its four boundaries.

Common Road (formerly Brown's Lane)

Houses on the corner of Common Road opposite Wheatbutts Cottage. Formerly known as Brown's Lane, this section of Common Road is one of the north/south roads that connected the original part of Common Road, the original residential road of the village, with the now main thoroughfare, Eton Wick Road. The houses are listed together with their occupants in the national Census of the mid-1800s. The first house built in the area (in the early 18th century) became an Ale House known as the 'Bulls Head'. Four other houses were added, and all are known as Hope Cottages. The different roof heights are an indication of the added houses. This photograph was taken in the 1960s.

The Common Road houses were refurbished and the exteriors clad in another outer skin of bricks c1970s. This photo was taken c1990. Well known 20th century inhabitants of the houses were Jennie Dowson and Maud Rivers, and their charity fund raising wares were always on display at the back of Jennie's corner house.

Eton Wick Road looking towards Windsor Castle

This postcard photograph dates to 1912/13. Bill Hearn's Saddlery shop (later to become Thames View Stores, and finally an Aquarium shop) is on the left. Mrs Hearn is in front of the shop entrance with her young daughter nearby. Ted Woolhouse is in the next entrance, outside his cycle shop; his daughter is pushing what could be a pram through the garden gate. The man with the wheelbarrow is Ern Brown. He is in front of Lovell's Bakery, beyond which is the Three Horseshoes public house. Note the flag pole, large tree and gas street lamp by the Three Horseshoes. The street lamp was then one of two in the village. Installation of gas pipes in 1910 allegedly killed the tree soon after. The allotments opposite the shops are now Haywards Mead. The modern photograph below was taken in 1994.

Life on Eton Wick Road 100 years ago

These two photographs were taken by the Rev. Demaus, who was village curate at the turn of the century, and an enthusiastic glass plate photographer as these pictures demonstrate. They are used by the kind permission of his son. These scenes of life on the Eton Wick Road (taken near the Three Horseshoes, the upper one looking east and the lower photo west), can be compared with other photographs of the area in the book. Note the unmetalled and very dusty road, lack of pavements, the horse drawn traders' traffic and the style of dress. The upper photograph shows Lovell's shop and Post Office (Ada Cottage). Both photos show the great oak tree that once stood in front of the Three Horseshoes. The lower photo shows the bay window of the Horseshoes, much as it is today, and likewise the Palmer Place terrace. There is no shop at Wellmans Cottages (later to become Thames View Stores). In these photographs c1900 there are no street lights. These were to come later, initially two when gas first came to the village and by the 1930s when there were 44 lights between the Slads and Dorney Common Gate. The elm trees in the background are lining Brown's lane (now part of Common Road).

Eton Wick Road taken by the junction with 'The Walk', from a photograph taken in the mid-1930s. The Village Hall is on the left in the distance, a view now obscured by the houses of Haywards Mead. On the right in the distance the Three Horseshoes pub sign can just be seen, in the middle distance by the hand cart the 'Meux's' stout and ale sign of 'The Grapes' pub, and in the foreground the Simond's Hop leaf sign for the Greyhound pub, situated at the Common Road end of the Walk. At this time Eton Wick Road was still lined with elm trees and gas lamps, one of which can be seen on the left. Originally, c1910 there were only two gas street lamps, the other one being opposite Ada Cottage. Clifton House (beyond the Greyhound sign) was at the time of the photograph Chantlers Grocery Stores and Post Office. Before the First World War the store was run by the Harmans. Opposite Clifton House on the Walk was another shop, now the site of Taylor Court.

Clifton House converted to residential use 1986 after many years as a shop. It was the site of the first school in the village. The Grapes public house sign now reads 'The Pickwick', and Meux and Simonds breweries are long gone. Harding's Cottages (between the Pickwick and Clifton House) are now the site of Clifton Lodge, senior citizens' homes.

The shop opposite Clifton House was originally a converted house on the end of St Leonards Place, a row of terraced houses running from The Walk to Sheepcote Road. The conversion to a shop is believed to have been carried out just after the Great War by farmer Harry Bunce for Mrs Godwin (later Slade) who lost her first husband in the War. It was the first shop in the village to sell ice cream (home made). In this photograph, taken in 1965, Mrs Challis stands outside the shop, which was then in the hands of Paxtons. Before Paxtons, Mrs Colwell was the proprietor, and during the 1930/40s, Joan Taylor ran it as a newsagent and tobacconist. The shop was demolished c1986, and Taylor Court, a residential development, was built on the site in the early 1990s and was named after Joan. Joan Taylor was closely related to the Tarrant, French (Windsor Boats) and Woolhouse village families.

Sheepcote Road

A group of school children pose on the school playing field in the mid-1920s. The original houses of Sheepcote Road are in the background facing east towards Windsor Castle and aptly named Castle View Villas. Elm trees stand where Sheepcote Road flats are now.

This Liberal party rally group of 1906 is pictured outside The Old Parsonage, situated on the corner of Eton Wick Road and Sheepcote Road. At the time of the photograph it was the home of Jack and George Spearman who became well known photographers (in Eton and Windsor, respectively). Their house served as the local Liberal Party H.Q. during the 1906 General Election. The car, which must have caused great excitement in the village, possibly belonged to the candidate, Sir Arnold Herbert. The bearded man by the passenger seat is John Lane born in 1850 and foreman carpenter to Henry Burfoot and Son. John was a Methodist preacher and regularly walked to Cookham to preach. The building became the Parsonage in 1911, when the Church was granted the lease.

The allotments

Ernie Benham maintaining his allotment in 1993.

Ernie believed his family had worked this ground, opposite the Old Parsonage since the village first had allotments in 1894. Certainly his father regularly won many classes of exhibits grown here during the 1920s to 1940s period of Village Horticulture Shows. Within a couple of years of the above photo the lease for the allotments expired and the land was returned to agriculture (lower picture, 1998). Green Belt regulations prevent this area being developed for the foreseeable future.

Common Road, eastern end

The upper photograph shows the old houses on the section of Common Road between Sheepcote Road and the Greyhound with their back gardens and outhouses facing onto the Great Common (taken during the 1960s). Originally there were thirteen houses known as Clifton Cottages. They were home to many of the well established old village families. The more attractive fronts of the houses then faced south. The fronts of the Georgian style houses which replaced them in the 1970s face north (photo below taken in the 1990s).

Ye Olde Cottage

Ye Olde Cottage, Common Road (above) c1948 was once owned by James Tarrant. Albert Bond was the last tenant, before moving his greengrocery business to the new shopping parade in Eton Wick Road in the early 1950s. The house was demolished and new houses built (below). The tree behind the houses is the 1897 Jubilee Oak.

The upper photograph was taken by artist George Henton in 1895. He entitled it 'Eton Wick boys gathering wild flowers'. It was one of a number of photos the artist took in the area, now in the possession of the Leicestershire Records Office. It is thought that the boy in the front may be Bert Bond, and the right-hand boy in the group of three Alf Quarterman. Possibly the flowers were for sale, for example to day trippers on passing river steamers. The well-trodden path is believed to be the popular footpath (before the M4 was built) between Sheepcote Road and Chalvey which crossed the Great Common. The boys would thus have crossed over the Chalvey Brook bridge and are approaching Sheepcote Road. On the photograph of the Common taken in 1995 (below), this would place the path between the right foreground and the nearest power cable pole. During WWII, a series of shallow trenches were dug across the common from this point to the railway arches to prevent enemy glider landings.

The Slough to Windsor Railway

The first train into Windsor from Slough was on October 8th 1849, running on a viaduct across the Great Common and the Slads. The Riverside Southern line opened two months later. Both Eton College and the Crown opposed the first railway link into Windsor, initially causing much delay. In the event, despite College and Crown apprehension, the biggest effect was on the horse cab and barge traffic.

The first Slough to Windsor line viaduct was a wooden structure, depicted in the artist's impression above. Thirteen years later the wooden viaduct was replaced by the brick structure we are all familiar with today (lower photo), which has a total of 297 brick arches. In 1846, the G.W.R. paid £246 in compensation for their line crossing Lammas lands. Some 50 years later this money, with accrued interest, bought recreation grounds for town and village.

Broken Furlong/Stonebridge Field

The upper photograph, taken in the mid-1970s, shows the Broken Furlong cornfield as it was, and below, as a residential development, built in the mid-1990s. Broken Furlong Road runs along the east side of the field. The actual tract of land originally named Stonebridge Field is located some distance north of the housing development, by the old pumping station/Eton College Golf Course. In times gone by, the Broken Furlong area was possibly the local yeomen's archery practice butts, when regular practice was compulsory.

The Willow Tree pub, Eton

The photograph above shows an armoured car driving past the Willow Tree pub on the Eton Wick Road, possibly carrying supplies during the 1947 floods.

This picture, taken in the mid-1990s, shows the pub building (left) converted to residential dwellings and the old houses replaced with new, most, if not all being housing for Eton College staff.

Tangier Lane, Eton

Around the turn of the 20th century, families of ten to thirteen children were brought up in these small cottages in Tangier Lane, very different from the smaller families, spaciousness and tidiness of today. The rather dismal looking entrance to Tangier Lane from the High Street shown in the photograph on the left, taken c1980, has been replaced by a Teddy Bear shop. Further down, flats have been built for the elderly, together with larger, more expensive apartments. A number of the tenants of the old cottages were rehoused in Bellsfield Court at Eton Wick. The lower photograph shows part of Tangier Lane as it is today, after completion of the demolition and rebuilding work.

The Eton Cinema

The cinema was owned by Willis & Sons, cycle makers (located where Eton Garages are now). It was built before the First World War behind No. 53 High Street, Eton, and remained in business until the mid-1920s. The ticket price was 1d on a Saturday morning. The projectionist was Mr Carmen; his projector broke down frequently. For many years after the cinema closed, the building (above) was used as a furniture store, and later, as a meeting place for Christian Science gatherings. The new development on the left-hand side of Kingstable Street (below) replaced the old cinema building.

Old Eton

Named after a clay pipe maker, this court off Brocas Street was situated at the back of the Crown and Cushion Inn in Eton High Street. Some 56 people lived in two rows of little cottages. There was a communal wash house where no doubt the town news was exchanged! This picture was taken in 1895 by artist George Henton and is used by kind permission of Leicestershire Records Office.

Number 102 Eton High Street was once occupied by G Bargent & Son, Butchers and Dairymen. In 1904 the site became the Fire Station, and later the Urban District Council Offices. Note the old water pipe! Studio 101 is to the left, very little altered.

SECTION NINE

The Parish at War

There are two bronze plaques at the entrance to St John the Evangelist Church, Eton, commemorating 91 servicemen from Eton, Eton Wick and Boveney killed in the Great War of 1914–18. Eton Wick and Boveney suffered 34 fatalities; 33 are named on the 1920 Memorial Service Sheet pictured below. The village population at the time was around 1100 in total. A further 12 villager servicemen were killed in the 1939–45 War.

NAMES OF THE FALLEN AND THEIR REGIMENTS.

NAME.	REGIMENT.
Ashman, C. A.	Honourable Artillery Company.
Ashman, H. D.	1st Berks Yeomanry.
Baldwin, P. G.	Royal Berks.
Bolton, G.	Oxfordshire and Bucks L.I.
Brown, A.	Grenadier Guards.
Brown, E.	Queen's West Surreys.
Bruce, A.	Highland Light Infantry.
Bryant, T. A.	Royal Berks.
Buckland, F. T.	Queen's West Surreys.
Bunce, A.	Worcestershire Regiment.
Caesar, A. J.	Grenadier Guards.
Church, F. R.	Royal Berks.
Clark, J.	R.F.A.
Colbourne, F.	M.G.C.
Dobson, H.	Royal West Riding Regiment.
Godwin, C. F. R.	1st Life Guards.
Hammerton, C. W.	Queen Victoria Rifles.
Hill, H.	H.M.S. "Aster."
Hobrough, R. T.	Royal Engineers.
Iremonger, A. T.	Royal Berks.
Jordan, E.	Royal Engineers.
Miles, C.	H.M.S. "Vanguard."
Moss, H. G.	R.A.S. Corps.
Newell, J.	Oxfordshire and Bucks L.I.
Newell, J. J.	Household Battalion.
Payne, W. W.	Royal Scots.
Percy, G. F.	Royal Warwickshire Regiment.
Pithers, H.	Oxfordshire and Bucks L.I.
Quarterman, H.	Royal Berks.
Richards, A.	S.W. Borderers.
Springford, I.	R.G.A.
Springford, J.	Sherwood Foresters.
Stallwood, A.	2nd Life Guards.

The 58 Eton town fatalities of 1914–18 listed on the plaques at St John's are:

George Batt
John Beesley
Gerald Warre-Cornish
Albert Clements
Charles Clements
James Cowley
William Deacon
Alfred Delaperrelle
Richard Durnford
Frank Dolan
Frederick Dolan
Arthur Edwards
Harry Fidler
George Fletcher
Ernest Groves
Leonard Groves
Percival Hart
James Hill
Thomas Holloway
Percy Holtum
Frederick Hutson
Cyril Jackson
William Jones
David Lipscombe
Ernest Long
George Lyford
Albert Maguire
Richard Marshall
William Mead
Herbert Mitchell
Lemuael McPeak
Frederick Morgan
Arthur Munday
Edward Moseley
George Middleton
Herbert New
George Newman
Wilford Oldham
Stanley Page
George Parker
Henry Pardoe
Frederick Plaistowe
Edward Foss Prior
James Ridgwell
Frank Rowland
William Rowland
Henry Sable
Harry Sayer
George Sellers
Martin Somerville
William Sutton
Walter Troday
George Turner
Maurice Stroud
William Underwood
Frank Welch
John Welch
George Wilson

Unveiling of the War Memorial to Eton Wick and Boveney's War Dead, March 13th 1920.

The Guard of Honour at the four corners of the Memorial are village ex-servicemen Petty Officer G Percy RN, Stoker R Bond RN, Company Quartermaster Sergeant G Attride Rifle Brigade and Sergeant Harry Balm RAF. A procession of ex-servicemen accompanied by the Band of the 2nd Life Guards marched from the Village Institute to St John the Baptist Church for the ceremony and church service. The Provost of Eton College addressed the congregation. There were 34 names inscribed on the Memorial. After WWII, 12 more villagers' names had to be added to the memorial inscriptions. A Service of Remembrance is still held on this spot each year on Remembrance Sunday.

Dorney Common anti-aircraft battery site. The Nissen huts of the Dorney Common anti-aircraft battery. When the army left in 1946, the acute shortage of domestic homes caused demobilised local men to 'squat' and set up home in the disused huts. Their new homes and furniture were almost immediately ruined by the 1947 floods, when the residents were evacuated by boat. This picture was taken in March 1947. The huts were still occupied in the 1950s.

Three of the war-time ATS girls in front of their Nissen hut home on Dorney Common. The camp and the 3.7 inch anti-aircraft guns were located along the brook, starting immediately adjacent to the south side of the Eton Wick cattle grid.

The first territorial anti-aircraft (ack-ack) unit arrived on the Dorney Common site in June 1940. Other local sites included the tower mounted 40mm on the Brocas, Eton. This photograph is of the 564(M) AA. Battery stationed on Dorney Common during 1943/4. The troop manning the 3.7 heavy ack-ack guns shot down a German ME 410 on the night of February 23/24th 1944. The raider crashed in High Wycombe. A number of the service personnel, male and female, married local villagers and set up home in Eton Wick.

Councillor Archibald Chew, together with his wife Annie became Evacuation Officers for Eton Wick during the 1939/45 War. Initially there were many evacuees from London; Eton and Eton Wick had 578 children to find homes for. Finding happy homes for so many from very different urban back-grounds must have been a very demanding task. In Eton Wick, to accommodate the schooling of the village children plus the evacuees, a morning/afternoon rota was introduced, alternating weekly. Archie Chew had been a business man working in London and lived in 'Bryanston', Moores Lane. As an Eton Urban District Councillor, he was appointed Evacuation Billeting Officer in 1939 and was also given responsibility for the salvage of wartime paper, cardboard and metal in the village. Mr Chew served on several committees and was strongly connected with the Alma Road Chapel. Troubled with poor health, he died in 1943, and two years later his only son Clifford was killed while piloting a plane carrying paratroopers over the Rhine. Clifford was Eton Wick's only officer fatality of either world war. Archibald and Annie also had three daughters, Mabel, Sylvia and Joyce.

Mr W Pardoe

Bill and his daughter Ellen photgraphed c1942. As far as is known, Bill was the only Eton Wicker to have served in both World Wars and to have a Service grave. He was a cavalry saddler in the Great War, and at the age of 51 on the outbreak of the Second World War, with a son in the Royal Engineers, volunteered again. Bill had five sons and five daughters. Sadly, tuberculosis claimed Bill's life, and those of two of his daughters, including Ellen.

Stand down of the local Home Guard Battalions

King George VI, a keen collector of cap badges, taking a close interest in Eton Wick resident Private Alf Cook's 'Upper Thames Patrol' unit badge. The Home Guard was first formed as Local Defence Volunteers in May 1940, and were stood down in December 1944. The units local to this area included the Heavy Ack-Ack battalion, the 8th Berks. (Windsor Borough Batt.), the 9th Berks. (Windsor Crown Land Batt.) and 'D' stretch Upper Thames Patrol. To mark the stand down, the Windsor Home Guard Battalions were inspected by King George at Windsor Castle.

Alma Road Victory children's party, 1945

The end of hostilities in Europe was celebrated with street parties and other activities. Plans were made for the welcome home of local servicemen and women. To raise funds a dance was held in Eton College School Hall and a public collection was taken in Eton Wick. The Eton U.D.C. gave a donation of £75. Other activities quickly raised the funds for the 'Welcome Home' entertainment. To mark the occasion each returning serviceman of Eton and Eton Wick received a suitably inscribed cigarette box made by Mr Plunkett, a local cabinet maker. The children and organisers of the Alma Road Party (above) are pictured on the stairs and balcony of the Village Hall.

Broken Furlong Victory party

Flags and Bunting appeared in Eton as a two day holiday was declared. Bonfires were lit, including an especially huge bonfire built by College boys on Fellows Eyot. For many children the occasion was the first time that they saw lights in shop windows. Informal street parties and teas were quickly arranged for the children, with tables and chairs and often a piano being brought from the houses nearby. Street parties were also held in Brocas Street and Tangier Lane, Eton. The children were also given a shilling and an orange.

SECTION TEN

The Thames and Floods

The Thames, in all its moods, has probably exerted the greatest influence on the local area. Early settlers naturally established themselves close to water as a source of life and means of transport. The name 'Eton' suggests a collection of dwelling places surrounded by water, and 'Wick' meant producer or larder to the eyot or island of Eton. Sites of Roman and earlier habitation have been identified. The river originally comprised many channels and eyots. Until the coming of the railway to Windsor in 1849 the river was an extremely busy waterway with heavy barge traffic. As late as the 1890s there are stories of local schoolboys leading the barge-towing horses along the tow path between Windsor and Marlow. On the return journey they rode the horses back across Maidenhead Thicket, for payment of one shilling.

Residents had to endure regular flooding. In November 1894 the river rose nine feet, and two months later, the river froze over in a great freeze. It would have been impossible to dry out houses and possessions in such winter conditions. In the winter of 1809, six of the arches of Fifteen Arch Bridge on the Eton to Slough Road were swept away by high waters. Eton and Eton Wick became regularly isolated by water in such conditions.

The coming of the railway brought many day trippers from London. Early photographs show the Brocas swarming with picnickers and bathers. Drownings became so frequent that a mortuary was built in Eton Wick to accommodate victims. A regular pre-WWII summer sight was local men washing themselves down with a bar of soap in the river. The site of the present day swan sanctuary was the Eton College Boys' swimming baths, known as Cuckoo Weir and just downstream, the Eton town baths, called The Sandy Baths, where most Porny School children learnt to swim.

Boveney Lock c1890. Within 10 years of this photo being taken the locks seen here became the site of the present day 'rollers' for skiffs, and a new larger lock was built to the left. The lock house too had gone, destroyed in an unaccounted fire. The present lock house was built in 1902. Note the long wooden beams on the lock gates, necessary to provide leverage for the manual opening of the gates. Electricity did not come to the lock until 1965.

Boveney Lock House in the mid-1990s. This house was built in 1902 to replace an earlier one which was burnt down. The lock house island was used during WWII as a sport and fitness camp site for youngsters, mainly from the Slough area. Alf Spayne, the camp leader was the popular but strict disciplinarian.

Boveney Lock c1910/20. Lock keeper John H Kemp was reputedly a small man and is probably on the extreme right. During the 1912–20 period, a Boveney (probably assistant) lock keeper named Williamson gave village youngsters talks on the Scott Antartic Expeditions. Williamson had served on both expeditions as a naval petty officer. Taking account of age, etc. it is possible Williamson is second from the right.

Boveney Lock. The photograph is the oldest (to date) in the History Society's collection and shows Eton College celebrating the birthday of King George III c1885. The boats are in the old lock, now known as 'the rollers'. The present lock was built in 1896/7. The lock house in the picture was burnt down, and replaced by the present house in 1902.

The present Boveney Lock. The old lock is on the left, fitted out with rollers for the use of light craft not requiring the use of the lock itself, and a footbridge giving access to the Lock House.

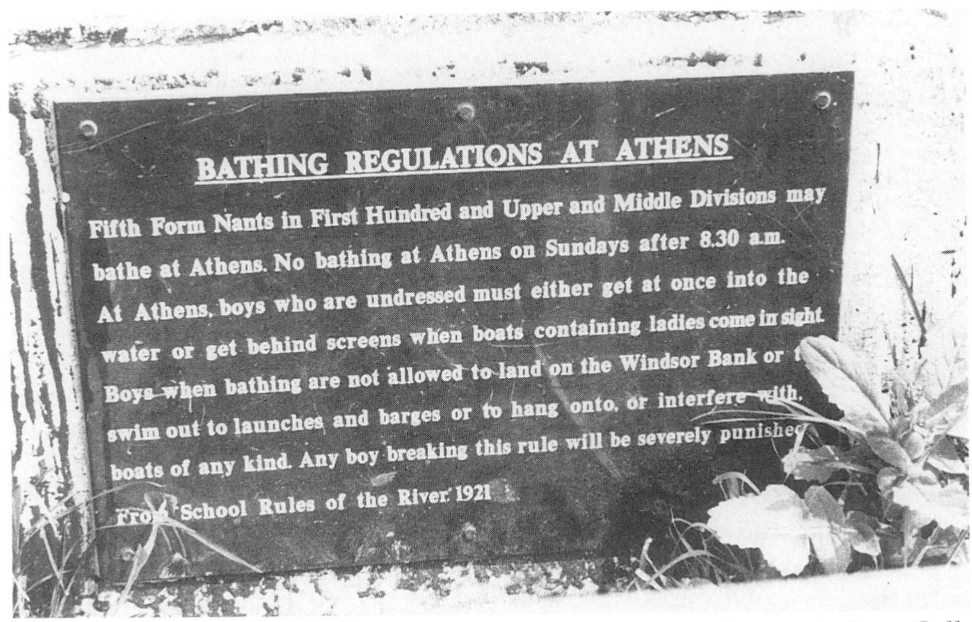

River Bathing at Athens. Before the provision of proper swimming pools, Eton College boys swam in the River Thames. One designated point is known as Athens. There is now a seat at the site, opposite Windsor Race Course and midway between the Iron Bridge (Boveney Stream outlet) and Chinese Bridge, and this plaque with some of the School 'Rules of the River 1921' is mounted on a stone block under the seat.

The Mortuary. This picture of the Eton Wick mortuary was taken c1960 just before it was demolished. It was built in 1913 on the north side of the brook running along Common Road approximately opposite Albert Place, sharing the entrance to the Blacksmith's forge. The occurrence of drownings in the river at that time warranted such a facility; before it was provided the accepted practice was to lay the bodies out in the rear quarters or cellars of public houses, where the subsequent inquest was held.

Pre-historic Thames Valley villagers. Eton Wick as a settlement is considered to have Anglo-Saxon origins, but there were human inhabitants in the area long before that, encouraged no doubt by the proximity of the river. This is a photograph taken during the 1985 archaeological dig in South Field near to the scout hut. The recreation ground is on the right of the fence; the tree line marks the river. This dig was sponsored by Berkshire County Council and the Manpower Services Commission. The team of graduates uncovered a historically important bronze age site, the first of its kind to be discovered in Berkshire and one of only 20 in the south of England. Finds included bone and stone tools and pottery estimated to be 3000 years old. In 1985 four areas of bronze age and iron age activity were discovered, and one trench produced neolithic flintwork, pottery and bone, including a comb of antler bone. The excavations were abandoned when funds ran out. In the 1990s during the ongoing construction of the nearby Eton College Rowing Lake and Thames Flood Alleviation Channel, the Oxford University and Thames Water Archaeological Units have made many exciting finds, which will be published early in the 21st century.

Flood Arches under the Windsor/Slough Relief Road. This photograph was taken around 1966/8 during construction of the road. Eton Wick Farmer James Kinross campaigned for the arches to be added to construction plans, maintaining that the road embankment would act as a huge dam in times of severe flood. The five arches have not yet been put to the test. In 1970, shortly after the relief road was opened, it was discovered that the Windsor/Eton Bridge was damaged beyond reasonable repair. The very busy main route over the bridge via Eton High Street was immediately closed to traffic, which then included heavy brick lorries and double decker buses.

The flood, November 1894. The photograph above gives a good impression of the depth of water in Eton High Street near Barnes Pool Bridge. This flood was nearly a foot deeper than the 1947 flood.

This picture shows Brocas Street; the Watermans Arms is at the end of the street on the right. The photograph appears to be artistically posed, with the residents in their best pinafores and polished shoes.

Eton High Street, 1894 floods. The floods in the High Street were very much deeper than shown in this picture. Possibly, the photographer did not venture out until the worst had abated.

Brocas Street c1920. Brocas Street, being close to the river, was prone to flooding, and the houses had stepped up doorways. Several of the houses also served as business premises. Although not clear in the photo, the small board over the left-hand window advertises the services of 'H Graver'. In the 1930s there were two sweet shops and a barber in the street. The reason for this large gathering of children in their wet weather gear is not known.

The flood, March 1947. Eton High Street with the 'Blue Bus' opposite the Post Office. The white sign points left to the wartime 'British Restaurant' which provided cheap meals from the Church Hall situated at the bottom of Sun Close. Behind the army truck is a Slough to Windsor double decker bus, a common sight (as were London Brick Company lorries) in Eton High Street until the closure of Windsor Bridge. For five days the water was too deep for the Blue Bus to use the Eton Wick Road. Its presence in this picture indicates that the floods were receding.

Swans swimming along the Eton Wick Road in March 1947 by Masters Field, Eton. The Willow Tree public house is on the left of the road, which then dips down to cross the Slads.

Flood water around the Broken Furlong/Somerville Road/South View homes was so deep that provisions were supplied by punt. This photograph was taken in March 1947. Gordon Paintin, then living in Eton and relief manager of the Co-op. Stores in Alma Road Eton Wick, waded the length of Eton Wick Road to open the stores, which were also surrounded by flood water. Gordon remembers the water being up to his chest by the time he was half way down the Eton Wick Road. Ed Bond paddled his kayak via Eton Recreation Ground to deliver his sister's rations to her home in Eton. The first four blocks of semi-detached houses built in nearby South View, to the west of Broken Furlong were the first local council homes, and were built in the early 1920s and allocated to ex-servicemen and their families.

The footbridge across the Slads during the 1947 flood. The sign of the former Willow Tree pub can be seen on the left of the picture. The angle iron support posts at the side of the footpath were a permanent feature. The planks and fittings were held in store for the then regular flood emergencies. Two posts have survived to the end of the century.

The Slads 1947. This photograph was taken from the railway bridge. The full length of the plank foot bridge can be seen on the left. The driver of the horse and cart may be George Paget who lived nearby, or Ted Quayle.

The nave of St John the Baptist Church, Eton Wick under the 1947 Flood water. Note the gas lights. Gas was piped to the village in 1910. However, it was 1935 before the church switched from oil to gas. Some outlaying dwellings were not connected until around the late 1940s. Electric lighting arrived in the village in 1951, and electric heating was installed in the church in 1958.

The March 1947 floods on Eton Wick Great Common, taken from Lords Close looking towards St John the Baptist Church. Behind the position of the photographer is Saddocks Farm, where the higher ground began. The flood water stopped at the front (south) doorstep of Saddocks Farm Cottages. Contractor R Bond's vehicles reached their yard at the back of Saddocks Farm via Bell Farm field tracks. This is a graphic demonstration that the Anglo Saxon Eton Wick was probably on the high ground to the north of the present village, where most of the farms are still located.

An R Bond Contractors lorry being driven along the Eton Wick Road past the site of the present St Gilbert Church. Norman Lane was the driver at the time. He used the lorry to take villagers to work in Slough Trading Estate via Dorney Common, the road via Eton being impassable for motor traffic at the height of the floods. Photograph taken in March 1947.

The Thames frozen over. The local stretch of the Thames has frozen several times over the centuries. Some older citizens remember talk of roasting sheep and oxen on the frozen river (not in the 20th century). These photographs of the January 1963 freeze show cyclists and walkers in the middle of the Thames. The large hut, situated on the Brocas, was used by the Eton Scouts until it was destroyed by fire. An anti-aircraft gun battery was located around this spot in WWII. In the lower photograph, swans enjoy being fed and photographed on the ice, with the snow covered bank of the Brocas in the background. Such was the thickness of the ice, there were no reports of serious mishaps.

SECTION ELEVEN

The Village History Group

This book has been produced by the Eton Wick History Group. Eight years old at the time of going to press it is probably the youngest group in the community. Originally the Group was intended to be a small core of enthusiasts interested in researching and recording the various facets of past village life. A inaugural meeting was held in the Village Hall in November 1991 to establish the group. Despite it being a very wet evening 46 people attended and it became obvious that there was need for something different and bigger from what had been envisaged. Since that initial meeting over fifty meetings have been held in the Village Hall with an average attendance in excess of fifty. A very wide and varied list of topics has been covered, usually of a local nature, as can be seen from the following list of programmes organised between 1992 and 1999. From the outset nothing formal was required. There is no formal membership; an admission price to the presentation/social evenings is charged to cover outgoings. Strict parochial boundary lines limiting presentations or research have been avoided. Neither is being born in Eton Wick a pre-requisite for joining in any of the Group's activities, as most of the Group can testify! Presenters and attendees from Dorney and Eton and even further afield have been welcomed at the regular meetings.

The pressure of finding and/or preparing material for the meetings has to some extent overtaken the original objectives of researching particular topics in depth, producing fact sheets and to record live interviews with certain characters. The group would welcome help in these directions. Nevertheless some significant projects have been undertaken, such as the refurbishment of the Folly Bridge Cattle Pound. The pound (on the Slads, near to the former Willow Tree public house) had fallen into a virtually unrecognisable state, with a large gaping hole in the brickwork; rubbish dumped in and around it; and the whole site overgrown with ivy. With financial help from the Royal Albert Institute Trust, Eton College and The Rural Action Trust, plus material help from Mr Hodge and Mr Savage of Andron Engineering, the History Group restored the 'Pound' in 1996. The following year at the Queen Victoria Diamond Jubilee Oak on Eton Wick Common, a new plaque was put in place, to replace the original bronze plaque that had been missing for many years, presumed stolen. Again, thanks were due to Andron Engineering for making the plaque. On another occasion the group wrote to Railtrack to express their concern at the state of the brick railway viaduct. In response, Railtrack organised a team of workers to carry out several weeks of refurbishment work (much still needs to be done). The late James (Jimmy) Kinross generously donated a sum of money to the Group, and in recognition of his kindness a 'Kinross Award' was established for the village school. Certificates are presented to pupils for their knowledge of Eton Wick, usually following a village walk-about and an essay. Books are presented to the school, with the names of the certificate winners written inside the covers.

To mark the Millennium the History Group has produced this illustrated book and the proceeds will go towards the costs of a three day exhibition of enlarged photos and memorabilia to be held in June 2000 at the Village Hall. All this was made possible by financial help from the Millennium Festival 'Awards for All' Fund and once again, The Royal Albert Institute Trust.

Eton Wick History Group Programme of meetings up to November 1999

03.11.92 Eton Wick – Now and Then
12.01.93 Farming
16.02.93 Floods of Yesteryear
14.04.93 A Walk Round the Village – No.1
26.06.93 Life in 1893
29.09.93 Boveney New Town and West of Bell Lane Southside Walk No. 2
10.11.93 The Commons and Lammas Lands
12.01.94 Herberts Supply Store, Eton
23.02.94 Eton Wick in WWII
13.04.94 Family Tree
01.06.94 After Herberts Store – Cullums Garage, Eton
14.09.94 Archaeology – The Earl of Cornwall
19.11.94 1914/18 War Casualities
07.12.94 Storms, Floods and Frost
11.01.95 Pubs and Punch
22.02.95 Eton College Rowing Trench
17.05.95 V.E. Day 1945
28.06.95 Characters and Benefactors
27.09.95 History of Boveney Church and Village
08.11.95 History of British Legion Poppy Appeal
03.12.95 History of Inns Taverns and Alehouses
24.01.96 Festive Evening. Local Picture Quiz
08.03.96 History of Dorney Court and the Village
17.04.96 Canadian Red Cross Hospital, Cliveden
22.05.96 History of the Thames Middle Reaches
26.06.96 History of Churches – Eton and Eton Wick
04.09.96 History of Local Council
23.10.96 Slough–Windsor Railway
27.11.96 Talk by Members – Various Subjects
22.01.97 Festive Evening Quiz
12.03.97 The Changing Face of Eton
30.04.97 The Influence of Eton and Eton College on Eton Wick
25.06.97 100 years ago. 1897 – Queen Victoria's Diamond Jubilee
July 97 Visit to Eton College Rowing Lake Oxford Archaeological Unit Dig
10.09.97 Eton College Rowing Lake – Talk by Oxford Archaeological Unit
29.10.97 Old Photographs of Eton and Eton Wick
10.12.97 The Old Christopher Inn
21.01.98 History of Salters Steamers
04.03.98 Press Gangs
15.04.98 History of Local Bridges
27.05.98 Village Shopkeepers – Past and Present
08.07.98 Local Fetes, Carnivals and Concerts
16.09.98 Decline of Local Farms and Horticulture
26.10.98 Archaeology of the Flood Relief Channel – The Thames Water Archaeological Unit
09.12.98 Group Members Exhibition
13.01.99 Eton College through the Archives
24.02.99 What Became of Trooper Ashman and Others? 1914/18 War
14.04.99 The History Of Burnham Beeches
26.05.99 The Changing Face of Eton as viewed through the Mark Bell Slides
14.07.99 Past Manufactuers and Craftsmen of Eton
29.09.99 The Fire and Restoration of Windsor Castle
10.11.99 Celebration to Mark the 150th Anniversary of the Slough to Windsor Railway

The Queen Victoria Diamond Jubilee Oak Tree Plaque. To commemorate Queen Victoria's Jubilee in 1897, Edward Littleton Vaughan, the village benefactor, planted an oak on the Common close to Wheatbutts Cottage. The original bronze plaque disappeared some time ago. In 1997, to mark the 100th anniversary since the planting of the oak, the Group organised a replacement plaque. The new plaque was made of stainless steel by Andrew Hodge and Ron Savage (Andron Engineering of Eton Wick). Andrew and Ron are in white shirts on the left, and in the centre respectively of the photograph, which was taken at the unveiling. Also in the photo are Mrs Joan Ballhatchet (reading plaque), Mr Tony Cullum (right). Mrs Everitt next to Tony, and Mrs Teresa Stanton is between Joan and Ron.

Folly Bridge, Eton Cattle Pound 1996. The photograph shows the gaping hole in the back of the cattle pound after removal of much ivy and weeds. Financial help was generously given towards repairs by The Royal Albert Institute Trust, Eton College (Lord of the Manor) and The Rural Action Trust. Under the direction of Ian Drummond, the Group cleared the site and contracted W Livesey & Son to repoint and repair the brickwork, to clear the interior and line the base with pea gravel on plastic sheeting. 'Andron' Engineering (Andrew Hodge and Ron Savage) removed the heavy steel gate, shot blasted and repainted it and refashioned the old lock before refitting. This latter work together with a descriptive stainless steel plaque they also generously contributed free of charge. The cattle pound was used, possibly up to post WWII, to 'impound' stray animals and cattle grazing in excess of their owners' Lammas or commons quota.

The James Kinross Award

In recognition of a generous donation to the History Group by retired farmer Jim Kinross of Manor Farm, an annual award was established at Eton Wick First School. Pupils submit work on the village and those judged the most meritorious are awarded certificates and an appropriate book endorsed with their name is presented to the school library. In this 1997 picture Mr Kinross is making the presentations in St John the Baptist Church. School Head Mrs Robinson is on the right of the photograph. Sadly, Jimmy Kinross died in 1999. With the School's co-operation it is hoped the Annual Award will perpetuate the memory of a great friend to Eton Wick.

Herberts Supply Stores, Eton

From his days as a youngster, History Group member Tony Cullum often wondered at the remarkable internal and external aspects of the grand building in Eton High Street which housed his father Ted Cullum's Garage business from 1927 until 1980. On the outside of the ornate brick frontage, there were coats of arms of Royal Warrants, and set in fine mosaics on the floor within the arched entrance from the High Street were the words 'Herberts Supply Stores'. On his retirement, Tony realised his ambition to research the history of the building, which by then had been demolished (in 1980) to enable High Street development and the widening of Tangier Lane. A fascinating piece of history was unearthed, around which Tony has made several very well attended presentations.

William John Herbert and family established their business in Eton in 1869. The building shown in the lower picture on the next page was constructed following a fire which destroyed the earlier premises on 21st June 1896. It was described as "the finest piece of Victorian architecture in Eton", and Herbert claimed it to be the "largest and best equipped store outside London". The Store at its zenith boasted 24 departments (plus a very special one at Christmas), and stocked thousands of lines (and virtually any item could be supplied to order), and employed 40 to 50 staff. It enjoyed Royal Patronage, including Queen Victoria and some 12 other European royals. William Herbert died on 23rd November 1906 and is buried in Eton Cemetery. The Store ceased trading around 1924/5. The picture below shows part of the interior of the department store.

The photograph above is of the grand frontage of Herberts Supply Stores in Eton High Street. The coats of arms are those of the Empress of Russia on the left, the Empress of Germany on the right and in the centre, Queen Victoria's, with the Prince of Wales Feathers on each side.

This photograph shows the Herberts Supply Stores building as Cullum's Garage, shortly before it was demolished in 1980. Tangier Lane is immediately to the left of the building.

SECTION TWELVE

Just Fancy That

This section of the book is a collection of miscellaneous facts and anecdotes from various sources, many of which may not be common knowledge; many will be lost as the generations move on. The 'Millennium' book provided the ideal opportunity to collate and record them. Many more similar snippets of information assuredly exist. If you, the reader know of any, the History Group would be pleased to add them to the records.

Boveney and the Crimean War

This item appeared in a publication of 1895. "I well remember the days of my youth when father anxious to make his public school boy sons happy, hired a farm at Boveney on Thames for a holiday, at that time a tumble down old Farm called Boveney Court, hidden among trees between Windsor and Bray. Eton boys feasted here on the Fourth of June and Election Days. I shall never forget old Boveney Court or its tiny church among the corn fields – a church then served every Sunday by a College Master. It was on the news coming down of the capture of Sebastopol that my father and brother and I rang a joyous peal from the belfry of old Boveney Church in honour of the English victory, much to the astonishment of the local villagers." (Sebastopol was captured during the Crimean War of the mid-1850s.)

Chantler H

At the start of the Second World War, Harry Chantler and fellow A.R.P. warden Archie Chew personally called at the homes of villagers who had not collected their government issue gas masks. Even then, one resident refused to accept his mask. In desperation Archie said to Harry "We will note this address, and if Eton Wick suffers a gas attack one of us will call again to see if he has changed his mind."

Church Bells

Just as beacons were used in olden times to warn of danger, or at a time of rejoicing, so too were church bells used. Bells were not used during the Second World War, but were rung to celebrate victory at the end of it in 1945. Church bells were also used to announce deaths in the village. A series of three tolls denoted the death of a man, two for a woman and one for a child. Lock keeper David Gibson, who does much voluntary work to keep Boveney Church tidy, rang the Boveney Church bells at midday on January 1st, the year 2000 to proclaim the new millennium.

Football

The boys' annual five-a-side football competition was traditionally played on Easter Sundays in the village recreation ground. The competition was followed in the afternoon by an adult match or other field entertainment. The special event in c1932/3 was a giant pushball match. A strong wind blew the ball away, followed by a large crowd, running towards Eton. They finally got it under control when it was stopped by the railway viaduct, about a mile away across South Field.

Football results

In the days of keen inter-village rivalry, the results of certain key matches were anxiously awaited. On at least one occasion when 'the Wick' was playing away against Datchet, a pigeon was released as goals were scored. Mobile phones are not the only answer.

Medical Services

When the village had its own resident nurse, she was accommodated in a thatched bungalow on the east side of Wheatbutts Field. Almost invariably, when would be patients called at her home she would be out visiting. A black board and chalk was left at the door for the caller to leave their message.

Ponds

The largest pond in Eton Wick was a short distance east from the Jubilee Oak that stands on the common in front of Dairy Farm. Once a year a motor cycle club rode through the side of the pond as one of the obstacles on their scramble course. On the last occasion it was held (in the mid-1930s) two local youths observed a surveyor measuring the depth of water. Knowing this to be the prelude to the afternoon scramble, the boys dammed the pond outlet stream. By the time of the scramble the water was almost a foot deeper. One after the other the motorbikes sputtered to a waterlogged halt. Could this have been the reason for it being the last scramble through the village?

Lammas Rights

In 1846 a Mr T Hughes was obliged to remove two dwellings he had built on his own land, which was however subject to Lammas Rights and which he had ignored. It is believed the site was near to the present Scout Hut.

Marriages

Following the building of St John the Evangelist Church, and while the College Chapel was still the Parish Church, the local authority wrongly thought that they could legally solemnise marriages in their new church. Between 1858 and 1875 there were some 223 such marriage services conducted before the error struck the townsfolk when in 1875 the daily newspapers reported that the Bishop of Oxford had introduced a Bill in the House of Lords to legalise the marriages. Few had thought that they had not been legally married, and the Bill was carried, probably before anybody had considered taking advantage of the loophole.

Mortuary

An abbreviated extract from the Windsor Express of 20th April 1901, concerning village blacksmith drowning:

Juryman:	There is a cemetery mortuary here, is there not?
Coroner:	I have never heard of one.
Mr Gill:	We have no mortuary, when we have a body and a publican will not take it, we place it in the church vestry.
Publican:	I don't mind sir, only the neighbours complain.
Juryman:	Is not a publican obliged to take them in? (bodies)
Coroner:	No, but I have authority to pay the publican 5 shillings to do so. It is very good of publicans to take them in.
Publican:	The body in question was not healthy.
Foreman:	I understand the body should lay at the George Inn (Eton) until Monday but thought it should not.

All seemed to agree on the necessity for a mortuary. One was built in Eton Wick 12 years later.

Pig keeping

In 1917, several villagers kept a pig, and it was suggested that a pig club should be formed. Mr E L Vaughan repeated an earlier offer to place a sow, free of charge at the disposal of the pig keepers.

Tic Tac

Sports reporters used to sit in the bedrooms of the Grapes pub (now the Pickwick) with telescopes on tripods, getting the results of the horse races on Windsor Race Course (across the river approximately a mile from the pub) from colleagues on the course. They would then telephone the results in from the pub.

Traffic calming

In 1919 it was proposed by the village that cars should be limited to 10 m.p.h. through Eton Wick.

Vaughan, Edward Littleton (1851–1940)

E L Vaughan's memorial inscription in Eton Cemetery reads: "BLESSED ARE THE PURE IN HEART FOR THEY SHALL SEE GOD ALSO HIS WIFE DOROTHEA JANE" (1865–1954). A full stop may have helped.

Urquhart

Farmer Urquhart (Manor Farm during World War II) was noted for his petulance. The village policeman had occasion to inspect the milk produced on the farm. Annoyance overcame Urquhart and as the policeman bent forward to inspect a pail of milk, Urquhart invited him "to have a closer look" and poured the milk over the policeman's head. On this occasion, prosecution followed.

Vandalism

Vandalism is often associated with present day youth; however, even in wartime 1942 the local paper contained a report headed "Vandalism at Boveney". River bathers had used Boveney Church to change in. It is not known if any damage was done, but since that time the Church has been kept locked.

Vandalism

Today, it is not an uncommon sight to see people or their children walking into corn fields, or throwing sticks in for their dogs to chase. In 1918, three village boys aged between 10 and 12 went into the corn in Wheatbutts Field to retrieve their ball. At their subsequent court appearance they were bound over for good behaviour, placed on probation and their parents fined 6 shillings and sixpence (a week's wages in 1918?).

Wartime Civilian Casualty

It is believed that the only wartime civilian casualty was A.R.P. Warden Bert Bond. On the night in question he was on duty as incendiary bombs rained down on the allotments off Sheepcote Road. He observed one go through the school roof and burn fiercely in the classroom. Bert climbed a wall of sandbags in front of the high window of the old building and used another sandbag to break in. A colleague tried the door, and found it unlocked, as it always was then for such a wartime emergency. The sequel was a needlessly cut hand for Bert, and, as it was wartime, a lengthy and difficult process to replace the glass.

Appendix A

Chronology of Events

1797	22 Cottages in Eton Wick, 10 between the Wheatbutts and Sheepcote.
1801	Eton and Eton Wick population (excluding College boys) was 2026.
1803	Threat of Napoleonic invasion; 200 parishioners volunteer for service, 42 selected.
1809	Floods sweep away 6 arches of Fifteen Arch Bridge.
1811	A recorded meeting of the Eton Wick Friendly Society, held at the Three Horseshoes.
1813	Eton Porny School built (this first building is now the Eton Ex-Servicemen's Club).
1822	New cast iron bridge across the Thames from Eton to Windsor.
1833	The Greyhound pub and the Thatched Cottage built.
1833	First licensed beer houses, the Shepherds Hut and the Greyhound.
1834	The Grapes (now the Pickwick) first licensed.
1838	First lock built at Boveney.
1840	Eton Wick School room (29 x 21 ft.) built at the top of The Walk.
1840	Principal landowners (acres): Manor 234, Crown 215 and College 114.
1842	The open sewer (Black Ditch) in Eton covered in.
1848	Railway pay £246 as compensation for viaduct crossing lammas lands.
1849	First train to enter Windsor over the then wooden viaduct.
1849	Eton Urban Sanitary Authority established (excluded the village).
1851	Eton Wick School room licensed for Divine Services.
1852	Prince Albert lays foundation stone for St John the Evangelist Church, Eton.
1854	St John the Evangelist Church consecrated.
1861	Census for Eton Wick lists 217 males and 233 females.
1863	Porny School built on new site.

1866	Queen Victoria donates Crown Land and £100 for construction of Church at Eton Wick.
1867	St John the Evangelist Church, Eton Wick consecrated.
1868	New building for Eton Porny School.
1870	Council purchase Bell Farm for Sanitary Farm purposes.
1875	Eton St John Church becomes the Parish Church (formerly the College Chapel).
1875	Council sell 9 acres of Bell Farm, which is later developed as Boveney New Town.
1878	Record of Lovells Bakery and Groceries Shop in Ada Cottage.
1878	Political rally and steam circus held on Great Common.
1878	Eton Wick holds its first Horticultural Society Show.
1878	First issue of the Eton Parish Magazine.
1880	A 'Penny bank' formed in the village.
1881	Eton Wick population 262 males and 258 females.
1883	Eton Poor Estate pay for a nurse to attend the poor.
1883	Infectious Diseases Hospital opened between Bell and Saddocks Farms. Eight beds. Not for villagers.
1884	Christy Minstrel Show in Eton Wick School oraganised by the Temperance Guild to raise funds for a drum and fife band.
1885	Village Working Men's and Young Men's Club formed.
1886	Eton Wick Temperance Guild has 18 adult and 63 child members.
1886	Primitive Methodist Chapel built in Alma Road.
1886	Queen Victoria donates half an acre and £100 for new school in Sheepcote Road.
1888	First Parish allotments (opposite College Sanatorium) with 40 plots of 10 poles each.
1888	Children's stained glass window dedicated in St John the Baptist Church.
1889	New village school opened. Cost £1000.
1889	Eton Wick Cricket Club formed. Early matches played on the Common.
1889	Old village school building used as an Institute.
1890	Eton opens a branch of the Mothers' Union.
1891	Eton holds Horticultural Show at College Eyot.

1892 Village gets its first own curate.

1892 Piped water comes to the village; shared taps.

1892 After 25 years the village church yard is consecrated and first burial there.

1892 Agreement with Burnham for spiritual care of Boveney New Town by Eton.

1893 Measles epidemic closes village school for one week.

1894 Land acquired for first village allotments south west of the church.

1894 Eton Wick now a Parish for civil purposes with its own Council of five.

1894 Boveney New Town now a Parish for civil purposes with its own Council of five.

1894 Highest recorded local floods force families to move upstairs.

1896 Windsor Bridge free of tolls.

1896/7 Larger locks built at Boveney.

1897 St John the Baptist Church licensed for marriages.

1899 Village boys and girls enter Windsor singing contest. (Band of Hope Shield).

1899 Church Lads Brigade company formed in Eton.

1899 Reservists recalled after outbreak of Boer War.

1900 Eton Wick win Berks. and Bucks. Junior Football Shield. Supper at the Three Horseshoes.

1900 Village forms branch of the Church Lads Brigade with 18 members.

1901 Village Rifle Club compete at Bisley.

1901 Lantern slides (Britons v Boers) in Institute. Door receipts 9/1d.

1902 Following a fire, new Lock Keeper's house built at Boveney.

1902 Pratts of Eton build a new shop on old village school site.

1902 First meeting of the Eton Wick Mothers' Union. (Attended by 70 people.)

1902 Renewed attempt with village Church Lads Brigade; 15 boys.

1902 Houses built along The Walk; probably the first to get piped tap water.

1903 Old village school building demolished.

1903 Village school to start night classes for lads to improve knowlege of reading, writing, arithmetic, history, geography and nature.

1904 Twenty-eight pupils attending the night classes.

1904 Pratts open first purpose built shop in the village.

1904 Heavy flooding again. Thames 5ft. above norm.

1904	Land levelled for a football pitch and cricket square.
1904	Eton Fire Station moved, site later to become site of Eton Council Offices.
1907	Eton Wick and Boveney Institute (now Village Hall) opened.
1907	Cycle shop (Ted Woolhouse) opens in the village.
1907	Eton Wick Harriers formed by E L Vaughan.
1908	Harmans take over Pratts shop.
1908	Harrier Club member runs in first Windsor to London Marathon.
1910	Gas piped to the village.
1912	Fire ladder and hose for public use attached to village stores.
1913	Harmans sell Clifton Stores. Post Office transfers to Clifton Stores.
1913	Mortuary built on Wheelwrights Piece, Common Road.
1914	First village fatal casuality of Great War; 4th September Sgt. A Caesar.
1915	Infant Welfare Group started in Eton Wick Institute.
1919	E L Vaughan purchases the Wheatbutts from the Eton Poor Estate.
1920	March 13th: the village War Memorial to 34 fatalities is unveiled.
1920	First year of Boys' five-a-side football competition for sons of ex-servicemen.
1922	Eton Wick Cricket Club move from Common to Saddocks Farm.
1922	Believed to be first year of village bus service – the Blue Bus.
1926	Eton Church Hall, Sun Lane built.
1926	Village Scout troop reformed; the College offers second hand uniforms.
1927	Village Girl Guides formed.
1928	Large elms along the Eton Wick Road removed.
1929	Uxbridge Gas Co. opens depot in Alma Road; manager A N Harding.
1929	Chantlers take over village store and sub post office.
1930	New wood-built scout hut opened in north west corner of the Wheatbutts field.
1930	Village Wolf Cub pack formed with Miss Clatworthy as Akela.
1930/1	Village Hall enlarged.
1932	Mr Chantler dies and son Harry takes over the Stores and sub post office.
1933	Eton Wick and Boveney Women's Institute formed.
1934	Eton Wick and Boveney Councils dissolved; now part of Eton Urban District Council.
1935	Gas replaces oil lamps in St John the Baptist Church.

1935	E L Vaughan starts the Boys Club in the Institute.
1936	Start of main drainage through the village.
1938	E L Vaughan gives part of the Wheatbutts field to eliminate a dangerous bend in the Eton Wick Road.
1939	September: Ragstone Road School opens and older village boys attend it instead of Porny School.
1939	War Evacuees arrive from London.
1940	E L 'Toddy' Vaughan dies aged 89.
1940	Village Hall used for Evacuees' schooling.
1940	Smoke emitting chimneys installed along the village road to screen Slough Estates from air attacks.
1941	April 14th: Incendiary bombs fall on village school.
1940/2	College purchases farms from Crown and becomes Lord of the Manor.
1942	Gas heating installed in St John the Baptist Church.
1944/5	David Niven, film star and army officer, resides in the Wheatbutts.
1945	Twelve pre-fabricated houses built on Bell Farm Field.
1946	New Youth Club for village 15 to 21 year olds formed.
1946	Village Scout Movement revised for the third time.
1947	Major flooding in Thames Valley. Dorney Camp squatters evacuated.
1948	Lord of the Manor, the College, holds Court Leet and appoints Lammas Officers.
1948	Extensive new building; Boveney New Road, Colenorton Crescent and Police Houses.
1949	Electricity belatedly comes to Eton Wick.
1950	Broken Furlong gets electricity.
1950	WWII Memorial built and unveiled on Eton Wick Recreation Ground.
1951	Electric lighting installed in St John the Baptist Church.
1951	Village's first shopping parade of seven shops, built on Meux Field, opens.
1951	Dorothea Vaughan leaves a stained glass window to Eton Wick Church in memory of her late husband.
1952	Stockdales Road Children's Recreation Ground opened by the Duke of Edinburgh.
1953	Eton's St John the Evangelist Church loses last remains of former spire.

1957	Windsor/Eton Bridge declared structurally unsafe and 12 ton limit imposed.
1958	Electric heating installed in village church.
1959	Wheatbutts elms felled and Eton Wick Road straightened.
1960	New brick built Scout Hut opened at Haywards Mead.
1962	New Village Hall extension covers in the stairs and balcony.
1963	Eton Women's Fellowship formed (following Mother's Union break up)
1964	St Gilbert Roman Catholic Church built at cost of £16,000 plus £1500 for the land.
1965	Eton Wick School extended again.
1967	First of 15 'Wicko' Carnivals held in old village recreation ground.
1970	The building formerly housing the Doctors Surgery and before that the Gas Depot in Alma Road is demolished.
1970	Windsor/Eton Bridge is closed to all vehicular traffic.
1972	Village Church Yard Scheme started to improve and maintain the grounds.
1973	Second village parade of Council shops opens in Bell Lane.
1977	Thames View Stores ceases trading as a grocers.
1980/2	Old elm tree hedge along village church yard replaced by beech.
1981	Wheatbutts Field development of houses and flats.
1983	Village Hall Boundary brick wall built.
1984	Archaeological dig east of village recreation ground.
1984	Grapes public house renamed 'The Pickwick'.
1985	Second archaeological dig between Scout Hut and recreation ground.
1985	After more than 70 years, village sub Post Office moves to Bell Lane Shopping parade.
1987	Old Post Office and Village Stores ceases trading. Fire Ladder is removed.
1988	After nearly 100 years of village trading, the Bonds sell their greengrocery business.
1988	Improved new weir (radial) installed at Boveney Lock.
1993	Chinese Bridge replaced with a new one.
1993	New Boveney Ditch (Splash) Bridge built.
1993	Brian and Vivian Whitty build and donate new village Church gates.

1993 Salmon Leap installed at Boveney Weir.

1993 Hotel Boat 'Actief' nearly causes major river flooding disaster.

1993/4 Further extension at rear of Village Hall.

1994 Aquatic shop, formerly Thames View Stores, ceases trading and is converted to private dwelling.

1994 Road chicanes installed east of church, by the Wheatbutts and by the Shepherds Hut.

1996 History Group (formed 1992) restore Folly Bridge Pound.

1996 Scout Hut destroyed by arson attack.

1997/8 Cycle track built from viaduct to Boveney Lock.

1997 Lease on allotments oppposite old Parsonage expires.

1998 Will Carling (England Rugby captain) opens the new Scout Hut.

1998 Roy and Joan Arnold retire – the last of the village butchers.

1999 Former Arnold's Butchers shop in original shopping parade becomes Hair Salon.

APPENDIX B

Map of Eton Wick and Surrounding Area

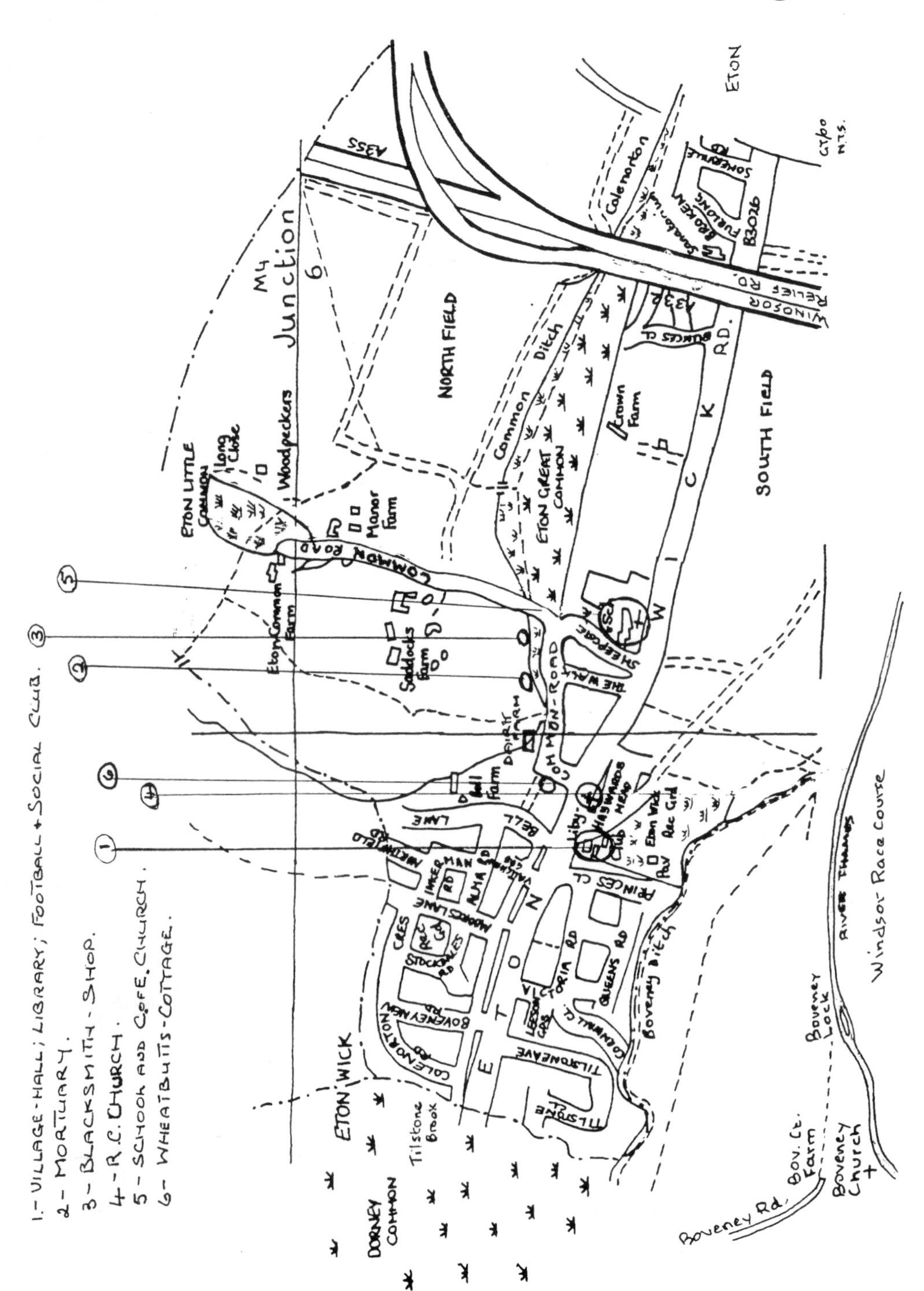